Leadership for Remote Learning

Learn how to adapt leadership and keep motivation alive in a remote learning setting or hybrid school. In this essential book, bestselling authors Ronald Williamson and Barbara R. Blackburn share frameworks and tools you can use to immediately make a difference in your school. You'll learn how to do the following:

- Navigate the change process in remote learning
- Maintain a collaborative remote learning school
- Address equity issues in remote instruction
- Communicate effectively across online platforms
- Provide essential professional development remotely

The chapter coverage ranges from school culture, to collaboration, to instructional leadership, to focusing on your own effective leadership. You will gain practical strategies and tips you can implement immediately to help your school and community flourish in a remote learning environment.

Ronald Williamson is Professor of Educational Leadership at Eastern Michigan University, USA. He is a former principal, central office administrator and executive director of the National Middle School Association (now AMLE).

Barbara R. Blackburn, a "Top 30 Global Guru in Education," is a bestselling author and sought-after consultant. She was an award-winning professor at Winthrop University and has taught students of all ages. In addition to speaking at conferences worldwide, she regularly presents virtual and on-site workshops for teachers and administrators.

Other Eye on Education Books Available From Routledge
(www.routledge.com/eyeoneducation)

**Rigor in the Remote Learning Classroom:
Instructional Tips and Strategies**
Barbara R. Blackburn

7 Strategies for Improving Your School
Ronald Williamson and Barbara R. Blackburn

Rigor is NOT a Four-Letter Word, 3rd Edition
Barbara R. Blackburn

Advocacy from A to Z
Robert Blackburn, Barbara R. Blackburn, Ronald Williamson

**Rigor in Your School:
A Toolkit for Leaders, 2nd Edition**
Ronald Williamson and Barbara R. Blackburn

The Principalship from A to Z, 2nd Edition
Ronald Williamson and Barbara R. Blackburn

**Supporting the Wounded Educator:
A Trauma-Sensitive Approach to Self-Care**
Dardi Hendershott and Joe Hendershott

**Becoming a Transformative Leader:
A Guide to Creating Equitable Schools**
Carolyn M. Shields

**Unconventional Leadership:
Bridging the Connected World with Meaningful Relationships**
Jessica M. Cabeen

Leadership for Remote Learning

Strategies for Success

Ronald Williamson and Barbara R. Blackburn

NEW YORK AND LONDON

First published 2021
by Routledge
52 Vanderbilt Avenue, New York, NY 10017

and by Routledge
2 Park Square, Milton Park, Abingdon, Oxon, OX14 4RN

Routledge is an imprint of the Taylor & Francis Group, an informa business

© 2021 Ronald Williamson and Barbara R. Blackburn

The right of Ronald Williamson and Barbara R. Blackburn to be identified as authors of this work has been asserted by them in accordance with sections 77 and 78 of the Copyright, Designs and Patents Act 1988.

All rights reserved. No part of this book may be reprinted or reproduced or utilised in any form or by any electronic, mechanical, or other means, now known or hereafter invented, including photocopying and recording, or in any information storage or retrieval system, without permission in writing from the publishers.

Trademark notice: Product or corporate names may be trademarks or registered trademarks, and are used only for identification and explanation without intent to infringe.

Library of Congress Cataloging-in-Publication Data
A catalog record for this title has been requested

ISBN: 978-0-367-68721-2 (hbk)
ISBN: 978-0-367-68863-9 (pbk)
ISBN: 978-1-003-13939-3 (ebk)

Typeset in Palatino
by Apex CoVantage, LLC

This book is dedicated to the countless teachers and school leaders who work tirelessly to assure students of a quality remote learning program. Your creativity and perseverance are surpassed only by your dedication to your students. Your work inspires me every day. Thank you for all that you do.

—*Ron Williamson*

I dedicate this book to the school leaders who have weathered, and are weathering, the myriad challenges of the COVID-19 pandemic. You were thrown into the middle of a crisis situation, and you continue to make a difference for your teachers and students.

—*Barbara Blackburn*

Contents

Preface ix
Acknowledgments xi
Meet the Authors xiii

1 Leadership for Remote Learning 1

2 Navigating the Change Process in
  Remote Learning 7

3 Nurturing Your School's Culture in a
  Remote Setting 37

4 Maintaining a Collaborative Remote
  Learning School 53

5 Communicating Effectively During
  Remote Learning 73

6 Instructional Leadership in a Remote
  Learning Setting 93

7 Providing Essential Professional Development
  Remotely 107

8 Ensuring Equity During Remote Instruction 123

9 Challenges and Concerns Related to Remote
  Learning and Leadership 139

10 Focusing on Yourself as a Leader in a Remote
   Environment 159

   References 181

Preface

What does your educational setting look like today? Is your school operating remotely? Or perhaps in a hybrid model? Or perhaps, you have, or are, transitioning from one type to the other? In today's world, educational leaders are required to respond rapidly to situations that are due to challenges out of our control.

After talking with leaders around the world, we heard one main question: "How do I lead in the changing area of remote learning?" This book answers that question by addressing key actions leaders can take in a variety of areas.

After discussing an overall model of change that can help with planning, we turn our attention to remote learning applications of three interrelated Cs: culture, collaboration and communication. Then, we will look at how to be an effective instructional leader in a remote setting, as well as options for remote professional development. Next, we will examine a critical issue related to remote learning: that of equity. This is a complex issue but one in which there are ways to provide assistance. In Chapter 9, we will concentrate on a variety of other challenges we face in remote learning, ranging from reacting to a crisis, to dealing with resistance from teachers, to parent and family communication and collaboration. Finally, we turn our attention to an often-overlooked topic: how to focus on yourself as a leader.

Throughout the book, you'll find practical tips and tools that you can use or adapt to your situation, no matter where your school is on the remote learning scale. You'll also notice a feature called "What If?" These are questions we often hear, along with our responses. It's a feature we have used in previous books that has proved popular with our readers.

As you lead your school and support all the internal and external stakeholders in your community, we would remind you that you are an effective leader. You are making a difference to students, teachers and family members, even if it does not always appear to be so. Continue to make a difference, and we hope the ideas throughout the book will help you become even more effective.

Acknowledgments

- Ron's wife, Marsha, for her love and support when I spend hours researching and writing.
- Ron's daughter and daughter-in-law, both elementary school teachers, as well as his son-in-law, an elementary school principal, for the opportunity to learn from those doing remote learning every day. We learned a lot from you, about both the benefits and the challenges, and it enriched this book.
- Ron's colleagues in the Department of Leadership and Counseling at Eastern Michigan University.
- Barbara's husband, Pete, who is always supportive and encouraging and who has helped me weather a year with the loss of two members of my immediate family.
- Barbara's best friend, Abbigail Armstrong. She continues to inspire me to make a difference with educators.
- John Maloney for a fabulous cover design.
- Autumn Spalding of Apex CoVantage, for her always superior production and design.
- Heather Jarrow for her ongoing support as our editor.
- Thank you to the hundreds of school leaders we've worked with in every part of the world. Your dedication to your students and teachers inspires us and all those around you.

Meet the Authors

Ronald Williamson is Professor of Educational Leadership at Eastern Michigan University. He previously taught at the University of North Carolina at Greensboro and was a public school administrator in Michigan. Ron has also served as the executive director of the National Middle School Association (now AMLE) and president of the National Forum to Accelerate Middle Grades Reform. Ron is the author of numerous articles, chapters and books on leadership and effective leadership practices. He's worked with schools across the country, including several large urban districts, as a leadership coach funded by the Edna McConnell Clark Foundation and the Galef Institute of Los Angeles; with suburban districts on a variety of school reform issues; and with rural Oregon districts on issues of college access for underrepresented groups.

Barbara R. Blackburn, PhD, one of the "Top 30 Global Gurus in Education," has dedicated her life to raising the level of rigor and motivation for professional educators and students alike. What differentiates Barbara's over 25 books are her easily executable concrete examples based on decades of experience as a teacher, professor and consultant.

Barbara has taught early childhood, elementary, middle and high school students and has served as an educational consultant for three publishing companies. She holds a master's degree in school administration and was certified as a teacher and a school principal in North Carolina. She received her doctorate in curriculum and teaching from the University of North Carolina at Greensboro. In 2006, she received the award for Outstanding Junior Professor at Winthrop University. She left her position at the University of North Carolina at Charlotte to write and speak full-time.

She speaks remotely and in person at state, national and international conferences, as well as regularly presenting workshops for teachers and administrators in elementary, middle and high schools. Both her on-site and virtual presentations and workshops are lively and engaging and filled with practical information. For more information, or to schedule professional development, please contact her at her website: www.barbarablackburnonline.com

1

Leadership for Remote Learning

A year ago who would have predicted that virtually every school in the United States would move to remote learning? But that was the reality in early 2020 when the COVID-19 pandemic swept the country.

In an instant schools were emptied and learning was transformed. Teachers and principals were immediately challenged to convert instruction from an intimate face-to-face experience to a more distant online setting.

Because of the rapid switch to remote learning, educators found themselves reacting to events rather than engaging in a more deliberate and thoughtful plan to move to remote learning. In too many cases instruction was a set of cobbled-together lessons anchored in resources teachers quickly found online, supported by sets of worksheets and other learning materials and including an occasional video or synchronous presentation on a video conferencing site.

Since then, we've watched as educators accepted the change, focused first on students and adapted their instruction. We applaud everyone for their work during those challenging times.

At the writing of this book six months have passed and a new school year is underway. All the signs are that districts have planned for a much different remote learning experience.

This book is not designed to critique the efforts of educators to provide a robust remote learning program, but rather to support those efforts. It is designed to provide leaders with strategies and tools they can use to immediately make a difference in their remote learning program.

No one knows what the future holds. Some schools have already returned to face-to-face instruction. Many have implemented a hybrid model combining face-to-face with a virtual component. Others extended their remote learning programs. In almost every case, when face-to-face instruction resumes, families have been provided an option for remote learning.

Starting the Conversation About Remote Learning

Over the past few months we've talked with countless school leaders. What's clear is that schools where the leader created a collegial culture were more successful when transitioning to remote learning. So, we spent time inquiring about the things that contributed to their success and organized the book around those issues.

Here are some questions those principals suggested as good ways to think about continuing to refine their remote learning program:

- ◆ How do you create a sense of urgency about the need to provide a quality remote learning program?
- ◆ How do you nurture and support a culture of collaboration among teachers when working remotely?
- ◆ How do we build ownership of our remote learning model among teachers, staff and the families we serve?
- ◆ How can we engage families and community in our remote learning program so that it has the vitality and rigor of our face-to-face program?
- ◆ How will we measure the success of our remote program, and how will we use that data to monitor and adjust what we're doing?

- What additional professional development is needed to support our remote learning program?
- How do we support families so that they can support our students while in remote learning?
- What strategies will we adopt to build support for remote learning among families and the greater school community?
- What adjustments do we need to make to the use of time, personnel and other resources to support our remote learning program?

What Is Remote Learning?

Across the nation there are a variety of models for remote learning. Some are entirely online with both synchronous and asynchronous components. Some are a hybrid of traditional in-school instruction a few days each week supplemented by online lessons. But the mix varies across states and school districts.

When we talk about remote learning, we're talking about the instruction that occurs when students are learning from home and teachers are working remotely. It can be a mix of instruction, including some whole-group teacher-led lessons, small online work groups and independent study. Students may be involved in discussions, watch short videos, complete online readings and activities or work on projects with other students.

There are key terms related to remote learning that provide a common base for understanding.

Terms Related to Remote Learning

Asynchronous Learning

Students access information and learn at various times. Typically, the teacher provides independent work, which may happen individually or in small groups.

Synchronous Learning

Students are learning at the same time, which allows for real-time interaction with the teacher. Video presentations are the most typical example of synchronous learning.

Gamification

Instruction based on gaming principles, including the use of point scoring, trophies and badges, various "levels" and leaderboards to increase engagement.

Hybrid Learning

Sometimes called blended learning, this is a mix of in-person and online or remote learning.

Learning Management System (LMS)

A software program where instruction and assessment are available. Typically, students are assessed and instruction is provided based on that assessment.

Social Media Learning: Social media learning refers to building of student learning through collaboration, discussion and creation and sharing of content through platforms such as blogs, wikis, Twitter and Facebook.

Virtual Classrooms: Virtual classrooms take place over the Internet rather than in a physical classroom.

Hybrid Instruction: A mix of remote, virtual instruction and on-site instruction.

The key to a successful remote learning model is that there is not one perfect model. Remote learning recognizes the uniqueness of every school district, every classroom and every teacher. While there may be constraints like the length of the school day or the adopted remote learning platform, teachers are encouraged to practice the "art of teaching" and continue to design instruction that is both engaging and motivational.

Challenges of Remote Learning

The swift transition to remote learning revealed lots of challenges. First and foremost was the uneven access to robust Internet services and even access to computers and/or tablets. In some communities, urban and rural, more than 40% of families lacked high-speed Internet access. It's a challenge to participate in online learning without this access.

But Internet access was not the only equity challenge. Families were immediately confronted with how to support their children's remote learning, especially when parents must work. Even when parents worked from home, they often found themselves competing with their children to use the computer.

Childcare and Internet access issues meant that a "one size fits all" approach to remote learning was inappropriate. Some students could not access a synchronous lesson and missed out on the discussion involved in such instruction. Accommodations were required for those students.

Few teachers had ever taught an online class. That meant there was a steep learning curve around technology, especially if the district adopted a new remote learning platform. Professional development and other training were often haphazard and inconsistent.

There will be other challenges. How to assure students with disabilities continued to receive services was a major concern. Similarly, there was an issue with how to address the learning needs for English language learners.

The good news is that America's teachers and school leaders responded, and there are countless examples of how each of these issues was addressed. That's the message of this book. There are solutions and there are strategies. Our goal is to discuss the issues more deeply and provide you with a generous supply of examples that you can use to design your own solution, one that appropriately fits your school and community.

Organization of the Book

Our goal in this book is to provide a variety of tools you can use, no matter where you are in the remote learning process. You may be using a fully remote instructional plan, a hybrid model or a fully face-to-face process. You may also be moving between two of those options due to changing conditions. We believe you will find helpful information, no matter what your situation. The chapters range from culture to professional development to focusing on your own leadership.

Chapter 2	Navigating the Change Process in Remote Learning
Chapter 3	Nurturing Your School's Culture in a Remote Setting
Chapter 4	Maintaining a Collaborative Remote Learning School
Chapter 5	Communicating Effectively During Remote Learning
Chapter 6	Instructional Leadership in a Remote Learning Setting
Chapter 7	Providing Essential Professional Development Remotely
Chapter 8	Ensuring Equity During Remote Instruction
Chapter 9	Challenges and Concerns Related to Remote Learning and Leadership
Chapter 10	Focusing on Yourself as a Leader in a Remote Environment

You'll also find a variety of charts and tools you can use to apply the concepts, as well as a "What If?" feature that provides answers to common questions. As you read the chapters, we would encourage you to think about how the material is applicable to your personal situation. You'll find questions at the end of each chapter to help you reflect and apply the information.

Final Thoughts

We're impressed with the way teachers and principals responded to the current crisis. Despite the challenges, schools quickly marshaled their resources to provide continuity to the school year. As mentioned earlier, we are not critiquing that work or suggesting that you didn't do your best. Our goal is to support your work by providing tools and strategies that will strengthen your skills and your remote learning program. Continue to make a difference, just as you already do.

2

Navigating the Change Process in Remote Learning

A critical leadership role is planning, whether that is for a return of face-to-face learning or some type of ongoing remote learning. Throughout the book, we have provided a variety of tools that you can use as you create a plan that addresses any change that occurs related to remote learning. In this chapter, we'll look at the four stages of our BASE Planning Model: Begin to Plan, Act to Implement, Sustain Success and Evaluate and Adjust. Prior to the planning process, it's important to build a sense of urgency for change.

Creating and Sustaining a Sense of Urgency

Launching a remote learning program can create a lot of urgency, especially when done almost overnight. But months after the conversion there's a fair amount of complacency remaining about the pace of conversion and the need to nurture and sustain the program.

Schools are not immune from complacency. Where most students are successful there is little incentive for change. Schools that are less successful often blame external factors like lack of Internet or insufficient funding rather than internal factors.

As we've said several times, we believe remote learning will not go away after the current health crisis but will continue to be a viable option for families in many school districts. In several states, remote learning charter schools are operating. Many traditional K–12 districts began their own remote learning schools prior to the current crisis and have made plans to expand those options in the future. And we have talked with district leaders who view remote learning as a viable option when inclement weather precludes face-to-face instruction.

Strategies for Creating Urgency

Perhaps the best-known advocate for urgency is John Kotter, a Harvard Business School professor and author of *Leading Change* (2012) and *A Sense of Urgency* (2008). Kotter described four strategies leaders can use to create urgency in their own organization.

Strategy 1—Break Down Barriers to the Outside

Most organizations devote their energy to sustaining current programs and practices. They promote from within, talk most frequently with one another and rely on others in the organization for professional development. Resistance to the idea that anyone from outside can, in any way, inform his or her work is often present. This internal focus limits thinking and can inhibit creativity and problem-solving. So, what does a school leader do? How do you respond?

Recognize the Problem of Relying on Internal Resources—Maintaining an internal focus means a school may miss opportunities for growth. It also means you may encounter hazards that will undermine your current program. Here's what you can do:

- Read widely from a variety of sources and gain insight into emerging social, economic and demographic trends,

both locally and nationally. Most importantly, read about trends in remote learning, even those with which you may disagree. Whether you like them or not, it's likely they will affect your school.
- ♦ Share what you've read and learned with teachers and others in your school and district. Talk about the issues but focus on the possibilities, not the threats. This will lessen the gap between inside and outside.

Listen to Employees and Families—Create an opportunity for candid conversation with employees and families about your school. Focus on listening, and be authentic in your response.

- ♦ Hold a series of online focus group or town hall meetings where you listen to what's working and what isn't. You might do several small groups so that you can hear from more voices. This can often be a tough conversation, but it is vital that you demonstrate your willingness to hear both the good and the bad. Take thorough notes and use them to develop a plan of action.

Options for Listening to Employees, Families and Other Stakeholders

Use of Zoom, Google Hangouts or Facebook groups for live discussion with small groups.

Use of questions and responses on a school-specific messaging board or communication platform.

Use of online surveys or response tools.

Email requests for information.

- ♦ Be respectful of employees and families. It's hard to engage either group when they feel distrusted or disrespected. Be candid and honest in all interactions. Be sensitive to the challenges they face due to the current health crisis.

Share Uncomfortable or Troubling Data—When you see troubling data about your school or you learn uncomfortable information, be prepared to share it. Don't shield employees from this information, or it reinforces complacency. Never blame the data or those who provided it.

Send People Out and Bring People In—Kotter suggests that you send "scouts" out to learn from other organizations about what is going on.

- Encourage teachers and other employees to participate in online conferences to learn about new trends and to visit schools that have implemented new programs. Expect them to share an honest assessment of what they learned.
- Organize a video conference with a team of teachers from a remote learning school recognized for its work. Ask them to talk about the challenges they've faced and how they overcame those challenges. Talk candidly about the benefits as well as the costs.
- Ask teachers to use their personal learning networks, which may include a variety of social media outlets, to gather information to share with the school.

Strategy 2—Act With Urgency Every Day

It's always been true that what leaders pay attention to becomes important. Leaders are role models, and teachers, families and students all note what the leader talks about, how the leader acts and what they pay attention to.

Respond Promptly—When you respond promptly, you're not hasty or act in less thoughtful ways. Rather, you know your priorities and you respond quickly with a well-thought-out plan of action.

- Respond quickly to issues involving priorities. A prompt response reinforces the importance of the issue.
- Be inquisitive about instruction in remote learning classrooms. In meetings, emails and other communication and in casual conversation, talk about your priorities,

ask questions about what is happening in classrooms and use every interaction as an opportunity to signal what's important.
- If you're participating in a meeting, make active engagement a priority. Avoid interruptions, and avoid leaving early. Never end the meeting without clarity about whom will do what and how quickly tasks will be completed.

Stop Doing Things That Aren't Urgent—Every school falls into the trap of doing things the way they've been done in the past. To do so can telegraph messages about complacency. So, change some of those behaviors and practices.

- Organize meetings and other routine activities differently. Modify the agenda. Use technology tools to minimize the need to share basic information in a meeting. Find ways to gather input from all and listen to the voices of every participant.
- Take control of your calendar and balance your responsibilities (more in Chapter 10). Purge low-priority items and projects. Delegate to assistants or teacher leaders. Create time to read and think deeply about the issues. Avoid unnecessary meetings, but increase the time you spend visiting online classrooms. Talk with both teachers and students, but more importantly, listen to what is being discussed.

Be Visibly Urgent—Because people pay attention to the leader and their actions, it is critical that you be visible and clearly demonstrate urgency.

- Be visible and accessible throughout the day. In a remote learning school that means time on your computer or tablet accessing classrooms. Don't be intrusive but be visible. Ask open-ended questions about the day and about instructional activities. In addition to being seen, devote time to informal conversation with teachers, other employees, students and families.

♦ Talk with passion about your school and your vision. Be relentless in talking about the quality of your remote learning program. But be prepared for people to share concerns about the program. Talk with feeling, and identify examples of how remote learning positively affects students and their learning.

Strategy 3—Embrace Crises

Crises are often seen as harmful with negative consequences. That can be true. Leaders often try to avoid crises. But some just happen, like the pandemic, and leaders have no control over them. But a crisis can also provide an opportunity to reexamine practices, to commit to new approaches and to adapt your school to a new reality. Moving to remote learning, while initially rushed, provides opportunity to rethink many instructional practices. It has more clearly illuminated many of the inequities that students and families experience (see Chapter 9). That provides an opportunity to address those inequities.

Use a Crisis to Create Urgency—Following any crisis, take time to reflect and focus on what you, and your school, learned. Use that reflection to engage employees and families in a discussion of beliefs and values, and identify ways to respond that don't threaten those values, but rather reinforce their importance. Be mindful that a crisis doesn't guarantee greater urgency.

Create a Crisis—Only partially in jest do we suggest creating a crisis and never do anything that might threaten your school or harm individuals. But you simply can't fail to act. Use data to shape the crisis or set expectations so individuals are forced to respond. Remote learning identified many inequities among families in most school communities. Once they are identified, the issue is responding to and addressing them. Just be clear that manufactured crises must be about "real" problems and not used to distract from "real" issues or tough personnel decisions.

Strategy 4—Dealing With Conflict

How you perceive roadblocks determines your response. Rather than seeing roadblocks as barriers, view them as opportunities. Richard Benjamin, a former superintendent in Nashville and suburban Atlanta, suggested that our critics are really our best friends because they force us to be clearer about our beliefs, to look more closely at our plans and to further consider the implications of our thinking.

That attitude can help a leader deal with what may appear to be insurmountable roadblocks: things that slow down or stop implementation of your innovation.

Constructively Deal With Conflict

Many improvement plans, like remote learning, never get fully implemented because either the leader or teachers avoid the conflict associated with the change. As we discussed earlier, not everyone will be supportive of something like remote learning. Some will openly resist. Many will simply disengage and hope the change goes away. Others may resign or retire rather than devote time to moving online.

There is no guarantee that implementing remote learning will be free of all conflict. There are, however, some things you can do to minimize and deal constructively with conflict. You might want to try the following.

Strategies for Dealing With Conflict

- Use data and descriptions to talk about issues, not value judgments or personal interpretations.
- Focus on the present, not what was or might have been.
- Own your own ideas and feelings; use "I" as much as possible when conveying your ideas.
- Explain, do not defend.
- Be attentive to nonverbal clues and messages in online meetings.
- Assume the motives of others are "honorable."
- Avoid the use of superlatives or absolutes like most, best, always or never.
- Agree when those of another viewpoint are right.
- Use active listening skills.

We've found that one of the most useful strategies for dealing with conflict is to build positive relationships with people. Although this can be more challenging in a remote learning setting, it is even more important. When conflict arises, you can draw on your reservoir of goodwill to help get past the difference of opinion.

Strategy 5—Deal With Naysayers
Every school has naysayers. They may be teachers or other employees, families, influential community members or even members of the administrative team. While they can't be ignored, neither can they be allowed to dominate the conversation or inhibit change. Don't confuse naysayers with skeptics. Skeptics ask questions, respond to data logically and often seek additional information. While skeptics can be annoying and slow down decisions, naysayers don't appreciate data or information and often suggest that no action is needed.

Don't Waste Time Co-opting a Naysayer—Naysayers try to stop action and have a tendency to disrupt conversation and delay action. They are often not inclined to listen and won't welcome data or accept decisions. Avoid their involvement in study groups and other activities designed to create urgency.

Never Ignore a Naysayer—On the other hand, you can't ignore them either. When ignored, a naysayer may create mischief. They are adept at raising questions that have an element of truth or overstating the problem. They often organize an active resistance, sometimes covertly, and sow dissention among members of the school community.

Distract the Naysayers—If you can't ignore them and you can't co-opt them, what do you do? Kotter (2008) suggests you distract them. First, find a special assignment or task for your naysayer. Ideally, that assignment will take them away from the core work. Second, pair them with someone who understands their job is to keep the naysayer distracted. Third, give them so much work that there is little time to create disruption and dissention. They still may find ways to be disruptive, but that disruption may be minimized.

What If . . .

Thanks for the ideas about naysayers, but what happens if they are the majority? Two-thirds of my staff fall in this category, and there are almost too many for the strategies to work. . . .

> If the majority of your staff are naysayers, it's an indication of a deeper problem. You should devote time to listening to them, asking them to identify the issues and probing for greater understanding. Naysayers often use resistance as a way to mask the "real" issue and conveniently grasp on to whatever you're currently working on. Meet with people individually, listen carefully and look for words or phrases that reveal the issue. Ask for solutions and don't settle for "just don't do it" or "let's keep it the way it was."

A sense of urgency is often needed to accelerate change and improve schools. Urgency is not created by a single event or through a single conversation or presentation. Rather, urgency emerges when there is a systematic approach by the school leader to modify the culture of their school. It starts with the leader and the way the leader spends time, the things they talk about and the priorities they set.

Planning Your Remote Learning Program and/or Planning the Return to Face-to-Face Instruction

We recognize that most schools moved to remote learning in response to the current health crisis. There was insufficient time for planning and little time for consultation or involvement by either the school's leadership team or even school principals. Often the decision was driven by mandates from state government or a decision by the local board of education.

We've also talked with lots of teachers and principals since their remote learning program began, and we have come to understand that resources were often scarce, professional development meager and programs felt cobbled together in order to survive the remainder of the school year.

We experienced some of the same effects. Ron teaches at a university, and one day the campus was bustling with students and staff, the next it was closed and courses moved entirely online. Barbara's niece attends a school that planned to be fully remote, changed their plans to fully online and is now using a hybrid model.

Those conditions don't allow for very thoughtful planning, just reacting. In the months since that transition, schools have been more considered in terms of planning. There's been greater involvement and more concern for the quality of the online platform for remote learning. We applaud those efforts.

We've observed schools successfully launch programs like remote learning, and we want to suggest a process that you can use to continue to refine and strengthen your current efforts. We believe it's critical to continue planning, to gather data about the launch of remote learning and to identify ways to address the challenges you identify. It's a four-step plan we call the BASE Planning Model.

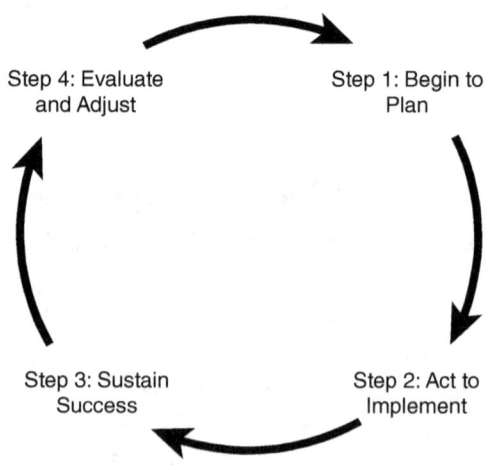

The BASE Planning Model

We've been involved in many planning projects and have come to appreciate that schools are constantly changing and improving. Sometimes the change is thrust on schools, like the move to remote learning. Sometimes, it's a more gradual process. We chose BASE because everything you do to improve your school must be built on a solid base, one that reflects research and best practice, builds support among teachers and families and includes solid measures for success.

The model provides a way to think about launching a new program and then making needed adjustments. It is circular in nature and assumes that to sustain improvement, you must study how you have done and that this study will naturally lead to identifying additional ways your school can continue to improve.

Of course, in most cases the move to remote learning was done quickly in response to state and local health conditions. There was little time for a collaborative approach or deliberation about the decision.

While that's not ideal, it's the way it happened. The first few months of remote learning, while rushed and perhaps not optimal, provided time to thoughtfully think about what a more sustainable remote learning model might encompass. In many places, their remote learning model continues to be monitored and adjusted.

> ***BASE Planning Model***
> ♦ Begin to Plan
> ♦ Act to Implement
> ♦ Sustain Success
> ♦ Evaluate and Adjust

Step 1: Beginning the Planning

We've identified some strategies that you can use to work with teachers, families and communities to develop or refine your remote learning model. They are much like any set of tools. Not every tool works for every job. Some tasks require more than one tool. What is critical is the ability to figure out which tool best fits the situation and will work most effectively.

Most importantly, these strategies recognize the importance of using an inclusive process that is focused on making remote learning successful.

Checklist of Planning Activities

_____ 1. Are critical stakeholders involved?
_____ 2. Is there an agreed-upon vision for remote learning?
_____ 3. Do we have the data and information about our current conditions?
_____ 4. Do we have a platform and a schedule that works for everyone?
_____ 5. Is there an agreed-upon process for making decisions?
_____ 6. How will we share information with others?

Use an Inclusive Process

Involving all stakeholders builds greater commitment to the outcomes. That is particularly true when you're talking about a dramatic change in instructional delivery. We've learned that when teachers and families get actively involved in discussing ways to improve their school, they are more likely to embrace the change.

The implications of remote learning on both teachers and families are immense. For many teachers they are teaching online for the first time. In addition to questions about the online platform, there are concerns about access to supplies and materials that may have been left in their classrooms and concern for student access and connectivity.

Families face a whole different set of issues. When parents work outside the home, there is a need to provide childcare. In remote learning, that may be an additional expense. Families may not have computers and robust Internet access for their children's use. And that's on top of the expectation that families will be much more active partners in delivering instruction and supervising student work.

As you consider change, be sure you gather information from parents and families as to their needs and perspectives. Although you will want to use online outlets for gathering information, that will not reach all parents. You may want to use some more traditional methods, such as phone calls.

Be Clear About Group Operations

We believe strongly in a collaborative approach and have found that groups are most successful when they have a clear process to guide their deliberations.

First, make sure you are clear about the video conferencing software you will use. It should be easily accessible and something that both teachers and family members can download and use. Zoom is an inexpensive choice for many school groups.

Second, believe that use of an agreed-upon set of norms about group operations and decision-making is critical. When Barbara works with teachers, both online and face-to-face, she uses a simple set of norms.

Sample Group Norms for Discussion and Decision-Making

- We are all a team, so we work together rather than competing.
- We respect each other and act appropriately.
- We actively listen to each other, which allows us to authentically contribute our perspectives.
- If you don't agree with someone, find a positive way to respond without embarrassing the other person.
- Everyone should be able to participate. If one person is talking too much, the other group members should give them a signal and move on.
- The process is just as important as the result. We want to think deeply about our work, elaborate, justify our points and pose additional questions to promote more thinking.

> - Making mistakes is normal; it helps us learn.
> - If you need help, check out the online Resource Board.

Garmston and Wellman (2013) also suggest a set of seven norms of collaboration. Information about the norms, including a self-assessment that may be used by any group, is available at www.thinkingcollaborative.com.

Be Clear About How Decisions Are Made

It is also important to be clear about how decisions will be made. It is much easier to talk about a decision-making process at the beginning rather than when a decision must be made. Consensus is always the goal, but occasionally that doesn't work, and groups need to be clear about how decisions will be made.

Deciding on a course of action can be a challenge and is frequently contentious, particularly if the decision is made by voting. Voting tends to create winners and losers. There are several other ways to make decisions. They include consensus, multi-voting or other decision-making tools.

Provide a Common Base of Information

Everyone involved in the work should have access to the same data and have an opportunity to look at the same print and/or electronic resources. Often, families, students and community members feel as though teachers and principals have "privileged" information. Occasionally, even some teachers don't have the same information, especially when someone shares specific content-area knowledge.

What If . . .

I can see how the members involved in the work need access to all information. And I agree that other stakeholders need some information. Should they have access to all information or just some? How do I determine that?

Never share data that would violate privacy requirements, but generally you want everyone in a work group to have access to the same information; otherwise, it appears that some members are favored and have greater access. That can create tension in the group that may inhibit your ability to work together.

Commit to the Use of Data

Groups that use members' opinions as the primary source of data almost always find themselves unable to make progress. We've found that the most productive groups are comfortable gathering and analyzing data independent of individuals' experience or opinion.

It is important to build remote learning on a foundation of data about student learning. Put together an online portfolio of materials that reflects the academic expectations of students, the quality of their work and the success on agreed-upon measures of academic success. It should also include any data you have from the initial months of remote learning. That could include things like data about student access, student online attendance and participation and information from any surveys of teachers and families or focus group discussions about the program. A shared Google Drive or a shared Dropbox would be a good place to locate this information.

We believe it is important to talk directly with teachers, families and students where appropriate using video conferencing software. You want to hear how people actually experienced the program. Don't get defensive. Welcome honest, candid feedback. Think of families as consumers, and listen closely for clues about both the quality of your remote learning program and ways to make it more "consumer focused."

Anchor Your Plan in a Shared Vision of Remote Learning

Any discussion about something as significant as remote learning must be based on a shared vision. A clear and compelling vision and mission reflect the collective commitment of a school community and serve as one way to link programs and practices to a common goal.

It's likely that when you launched your remote learning program you had no time to talk about vision. But now that a program is underway, you can take some time to talk with teachers and families about their experience and agree upon some key descriptors that would characterize your program. The International Association for K-12 Online Learning has developed National Standards for Online Teaching (www.nsqol.org/the-standards/quality-online-teaching/). Developed in 2011 and currently under revision, the standards focus on 11 areas that provide a comprehensive evaluation of online teaching and learning.

1. Knows concepts and structures of effective online instruction and can create opportunities for student success.
2. Understands and is able to use a range of technologies for student learning and engagement.
3. Plans, designs and incorporates strategies to encourage active learning, application, interaction, participation and collaboration.
4. Promotes student success through clear expectations, prompt responses and effective feedback.
5. Models, guides and encourages legal, ethical and safe behavior related to technology use.
6. Is cognizant of the diversity of student academic needs and incorporates accommodations into the online environment.
7. Demonstrates competencies in creating and implementing assessments in online learning environments in ways that ensure validity and reliability of the instruments and procedures.
8. Develops and delivers assessments, projects and assignments that meet standards-based learning goals and assesses learning progress by measuring student achievement of the learning goals.

9. Demonstrates competency in using data from assessments and other data sources to modify content and to guide student learning.
10. Interacts in a professional, effective manner with colleagues, parents and other members of the community to support students' success.
11. Arranges media and content to help students and teachers transfer knowledge most effectively in the online environment.

Planning for Organization of Online Instruction

Perhaps the most fundamental issue in remote learning is the choice of a platform for providing instruction. When many districts quickly transitioned to remote learning, few had an identified platform for online instruction. Initially, delivery was a mix of video conferencing like Zoom or Google Hangouts and materials that individual teachers quickly created. Things like short videos or emailed handouts characterized instruction. As you build your plan, there are two concerns to address: determining an online platform and organizing the remote learning day.

Online Platforms

There are many different kinds of platforms. All have advantages and disadvantages and reflect values about the use of time, opportunity for collaboration and instructional delivery. In most cases, this is not a school-based decision; rather, districts mandate a common platform. However, there are general guidelines that districts have learned about platforms.

We read recently that there are more than 30 online platforms. By the time this is published, there will be more. Two of the most common are Canvas and Google Classroom. But there are many other good instructional delivery models.

If you think of your online platform as simply a way of organizing teachers and students, it limits the approaches you may consider. We recognize that every school faces constraints in their choices. Things like student access to the Internet, teacher expertise or even the organization of your school can inhibit your choices.

Regardless of the platform, here are some things districts have learned about selecting an appropriate platform.

- **User Friendly**—Make sure the platform is easy to use and navigate. That is true for teachers but also true for students, sometimes very young, and their families. It should not be difficult to log in, find information or submit student work.
- **Lots of Options and Tools**—The platform should be compatible with a rich selection of instructional tools. It should be easy to upload videos and other information. It should be compatible with Zoom or other video conferencing tools, and it should be easy to link to information and resources located elsewhere on the Internet.
- **Flexible and Customizable**—Your platform needs to allow teachers flexibility to customize online instruction, just as they would in a traditional face-to-face classroom. It must also allow distinctions between early elementary classrooms and high school classrooms.
- **Assures Privacy**—Some online platforms are better at providing privacy for teachers and students. You should only select a platform with robust privacy protection that assures student data, including contact information and grades, are not shared with those not authorized to access the information.
- **Provides Synchronous and Asynchronous Instruction**—Good online platforms allow teachers to vary their instruction and allow for both synchronous instruction and asynchronous options. The best platforms allow teachers to record synchronous lessons so that students who lack robust Internet access or who are unable to participate synchronously can watch the lesson at a later time.
- **Includes Communication Tools**—The best online platforms include a way for teachers, students and families to communicate with one another.

- **Integrates Video Conferencing**—The platform should include an option for synchronous video. Video can be used for instruction and for interacting with students and/or colleagues.
- **Supports Community**—Integrated into the platform should be the ability for a teacher to organize breakout groups for small-group work and discussion. The platform should also make it easy for teachers to collaborate with colleagues and promote community among the faculty.

Organizing the Remote Learning Day

Just as there are many different platforms for remote learning, there are just as many ways to organize the instructional day. Most models include options for both synchronous and asynchronous activities.

Here are some things you will want to consider when organizing your remote learning day:

- **Set Clear Expectations**—Be clear about the expectations for students and families. That includes participating in synchronous lessons, discussions or work groups. At the same time recognize that families will have varying access to technology, including Internet access, and some expectations about participating in synchronous lessons may need to provide accommodations.
- **Establish Parameters for Contact and Communication**—Be clear about the start and end of the school day, including office hours for teachers. Just as in a traditional model, teachers are not expected to read and respond to student or family inquires 24/7.
- **Provide Training on the Platform**—Almost every district provides training for teachers, but students and families also need information on how to use the platform and navigate its features. Some schools have a designated IT contact whose job is to help families resolve issues of access and use of the instructional platform.

- **Balance Synchronous and Asynchronous**—Be explicit with teachers about balancing the two types of online instruction. Recognize the developmental differences between early elementary and high school students. Just as most traditional instruction is not totally teacher-centered, online learning should also include a balance of teacher-led instruction and individual and small-group application and use of their learning.
- **Allow for the "Art of Teaching"**—The very best instruction thrives in an environment where teachers know they have control of their instruction and can be creative in the lessons they design and deliver. Good remote learning allows for that creativity. While students thrive in an environment of consistency and routine, they also excel when they are engaged and motivated. Remote learning should promote rather than inhibit teacher flexibility and creativity.
- **Assure Time for Teacher Planning**—The remote learning day or week should include time for teacher planning. The transition to remote learning has required an extraordinary investment of teacher time to adapt lessons to the online environment. We've found that many districts set aside one day a week, often Wednesday, for teacher planning and collaboration. Students use that day to work on assignments and other work for their classes.

Step 2: Act to Implement the Plan

As complex as planning can be, implementing and sustaining a remote learning program can be even more of a challenge. It is the implementation that forces people to face the reality that things "may be different." The reality of implementation can provoke a range of feelings, including regret over abandoning familiar practices, exhilaration at the prospect of new ideas or of being overwhelmed by the complexity of doing something new.

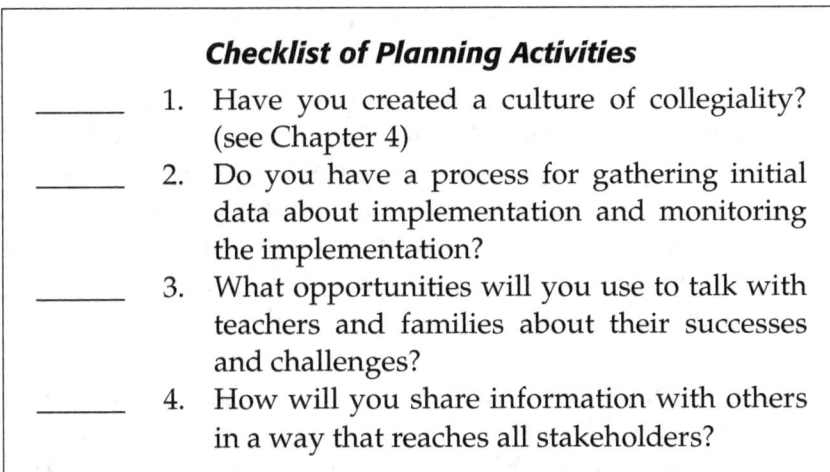

Few changes as complex as remote learning go perfectly when implemented. Even with ample time to plan, extensive professional development and sufficient resources, it is likely that some issues will emerge that need attention.

When this occurs, it is important to maintain a focus on improvement and not become overly defensive. We've found the following strategies to be very helpful.

Look at the Data—Gather and review any relevant data. In addition to any student learning data, we think it may be helpful to talk with groups of teachers, and families, about their experience. Look for patterns in their comments. Chapter 4 provides examples of ways to have open, honest and candid conversations.

Provide Time to Reflect on and Discuss the Issues—Provide an opportunity for groups or individuals to share their concerns and discuss the implications. Some individuals may want to talk privately, but we've found that it is helpful to have a process for structured feedback about an innovation. You could invite written feedback or arrange a series of Zoom meetings organized around structured discussion questions.

Provide Technology Resources for Teachers—Critical to the success of online learning is the ability of teachers to lead remote instruction. There are several teacher concerns to attend to throughout the action step.

- **Provide Ongoing Professional Development**—Few teachers had experience teaching online. The transition was swift, and teachers had to adapt quickly. The most successful districts provided multiple opportunities for teachers to learn about the tools they were expected to use and were provided with ample time to plan and prepare for remote learning. As with most professional development, it needs to continue. Often, you don't know the questions to ask until you're actually using the technology.
- **Provide a Help Desk**—Your district should provide an IT help desk to provide immediate support for teachers and resolve any issues with the online platform. At a minimum, identify a technology-savvy teacher who can support and assist colleagues. A middle school teacher friend from Connecticut always suggests finding a student to help.
- **Don't Neglect Privacy Issues**—Make sure that your online platform and any integrated tools provide appropriate protection of student and teacher privacy.
- **Google It**—If all else fails, do an online search and you'll get suggestions for a whole variety of digital tools and resources. Be sure they're compatible with the online platform, address privacy concerns and are easy to use for everyone, including teachers, students and families.

Don't Rush to Judgment—Be cautious about rushing to change things too quickly. It is very common for an implementation slump to occur. By that we mean that during the first few months of implementation, many teachers may still be learning how to fully implement remote learning. Don't rush to change things before you have sufficient information.

Make Appropriate Adjustments—On the other hand, you should never continue to implement a strategy that clearly is not working. If the data show that there is a need to rethink part of your plan, do so. Often, you may learn that you may need additional professional development, a more structured online experience or to rebalance synchronous and asynchronous learning. Stay focused on assuring that the implementation is successful and positively benefits students.

Establish Accountability for Results

Accountability is critical. It should not be punitive or heavy-handed, but it must be clearly defined and steadfastly implemented. While the initial months of many remote learning programs were rushed and hastily conceived, most schools have refined their program and strengthened their delivery. It's important that teachers and other staff recognize their accountability for implementing the program, for collecting and using data to guide implementation and for engaging in collegial conversations about their work.

As school leaders, we learned that it is important to continue to support staff during implementation. Few things work exactly as planned. It is necessary to provide support and encouragement and maintain a focus on the goal.

Continue to invest in professional development. Often important implementation questions emerge only once an innovation has begun. We've found that it is helpful to create structures that allow staff to share their experience with remote learning and support one another during implementation.

Step 3: Sustain Success

We've found that when you actively involve teachers and other staff in planning and implementation, change is more likely to be successful. It is critical, therefore, that leaders create a culture that supports innovation and creativity and builds capacity for continued improvement.

The third step of our planning model focuses on sustaining success. Earlier we discussed ways to monitor implementation of remote learning. We suggest you continue those activities. In addition, we encourage you to provide continued support for the implementation and begin to build internal capacity with teacher leaders so that a commitment to continued improvement of your program is nurtured and sustained.

> **Checklist of Planning Activities**
>
> _____ 1. Do you have a plan for monitoring the success of remote learning, identifying next steps and suggesting appropriate changes?
> _____ 2. Is there time for teachers to work with colleagues to share successes and participate in professional development?
> _____ 3. What steps will you take to create a culture that continues to nurture remote learning?
> _____ 4. How will you gather data and use that data to guide decisions?
> _____ 5. What is your plan for celebrating successes?

Continue to Provide Support for Success

You need to build a structure that supports success. Too often support declines after the initial flurry of activity. Continue to provide professional development for teachers, collaborative time for teachers to work with one another and supplies and materials needed to make the change succeed. One concern from teachers is that they receive professional development on a specific instructional platform, but they do not receive training on updates and changes. Also, every school year there is turnover in staff, and it is critical that new teachers be provided the opportunity to successfully participate in your remote learning program.

Monitor the Implementation—If you have not already done so, it is important to organize a group to monitor the continued implementation of remote learning. The group should represent all of the important groups in your school, develop the skills for collaborative work and be committed to using data to guide decisions about further program improvement.

Identify Time for Collaboration—It is important that teachers have time to talk with colleagues about their experience with remote learning. We've found that this collaborative time is one of the catalysts for nurturing and sustaining change.

Teachers value the opportunity to meet with grade or content peers to discuss successes, diagnose ways to improve and develop a repertoire of strategies that they can use in their own classrooms. Your school or district may have a video conferencing platform that can be used for these discussions, and any materials, such as student work samples, can be posted as a shared document for easy access.

Create a Culture of Continuous Improvement

The most successful schools are places where there is a collective commitment to continuous improvement. Teachers and administrators recognize the need to regularly monitor what they are doing and make adjustments to assure the success of every student. That is certainly true for remote learning. For most schools, this is their first experience with remote learning. Much can be learned from the experience, and everyone should be open to regularly monitoring and adjusting where appropriate. Most of all, teachers, families and students look to the leader for assurance that plans are thoughtful, carefully implemented and routinely monitored.

Use Data to Study the Results

There is often a tendency to make decisions about programs based on informal data such as people's feelings or personal experiences. While interesting, we've found that it is more useful to agree upon indicators that will be used to monitor your success.

Once you have agreed on measures of success for your improvement plan, you must routinely gather the data and use it to guide decisions that sustain implementation. Data are most useful when they include multiple measures—different types of data and when they are longitudinal cover more than a single year. Plan on gathering data about your launch of remote learning and its success in subsequent years.

Identify Successes and Celebrate

Effective schools celebrate small wins frequently. Have you ever heard the statement "Success breeds success"? It's true. Celebrating small gains on a regular basis can motivate teachers and students. Over time, small, steady gains add up to real growth.

Create a culture that celebrates authentic success. Keep data on school and classroom efforts, monitor their impact and celebrate on a regular basis.

Ideas for Celebrating Success

- Recognize teachers who made an exceptional transition to remote learning.
- Plan a year-end school-wide celebration to reward students and teachers for successfully navigating the transition.
- Talk with individual students about their academic success.
- Write a brief note to a teacher about something you observed in their online platform.
- Create social media postings and/or presentations about your school's remote learning program to be shared with parents and community groups.
- Tell stories about students and/or families who overcame obstacles and succeeded in remote learning.

What If . . .

Although we are in fully remote learning right now, we anticipate moving to a hybrid model, and hopefully back to full-time face-to-face instruction. How do I sustain success through all those stages?

The uncertainty about what happens next is a real problem. Acknowledge it to teachers and your community. Be clear about a commitment to regular, accurate communication about what happens next, and when you are able to transition to a hybrid model or back to full-time face-to-face instruction, take time to plan the move. It's clear that schools will not simply "move back" and do the same things. Some aspects of school life are permanently changed, like concern about cleanliness and safety. You reduce uncertainty by having a clear plan, and the best plans are developed collaboratively and the information shared widely. Confidence in the plan will reduce uncertainty and help to sustain your program.

Step 4: Evaluate and Adjust

The very best schools constantly monitor their performance and identify ways to continue to make improvements. The final stage of our planning model is to "Evaluate and Adjust." As we said, the planning process is circular. The decisions you make during this stage will naturally lead you to continue strengthening and refining remote learning so that it is even better.

As with the other steps, there are several important considerations. Because we discussed them earlier, we will not repeat them here, but here are some of the most important activities for evaluating and adjusting your plan.

Checklist of Planning Activities

1. Do you have a process to evaluate the success of your remote learning program and identify next steps for improvement?
2. Have you gathered the data to make informed decisions about your progress?
3. What plans are developed for sharing information with teachers, families and the community?

Data, Data, Data

Data is really important. We've mentioned it a lot, but want to be clear that decisions about monitoring, evaluating and adjusting remote learning programs must use data about student learning, preferably types of data that you identified early in the program. That data are strongest when they parallel the data you would use in a traditional face-to-face program.

Be clear about norms you will use to talk about the data. Avoid reliance on personal opinion or "experience." But be comfortable challenging the data, asking probing questions and identifying additional data that you may want to collect. Your initial data sources may not provide a complete picture or may have gaps.

Share What You Are Doing

It is also important to have a plan for sharing your work with teachers, families and community. Chapter 6 shares several strategies that you might use to communicate with your school community.

A collective commitment to remote learning is anchored in a shared vision and confidence that the plan is collaboratively developed. Your evaluation plans should strengthen this confidence through wide dissemination of both the plan and the findings.

Sharing Results
- Share the results with stakeholder groups.
- Acknowledge both strengths and weaknesses.
- Disseminate information widely.
- Provide time for ample discussion of the results.
- Use data to guide continued planning.

Final Thoughts

We recognize that most schools rushed to implement a remote learning program. That led to uneven implementation as teachers and school leaders grappled with the magnitude of such a fundamental shift in instructional delivery. We're not critical of the outcomes, but rather supportive of your efforts. As you move forward, we encourage taking time for a more deliberative, and more inclusive, planning process, one that is anchored in data about student learning and about the experience of teachers, families and students with remote learning.

No one knows what the future holds. But based upon initial data, we think it is likely that many school districts will continue their remote learning programs even after the return to traditional face-to-face instruction. Remote learning is a viable alternative for families and for students whose circumstances require something other than a traditional school setting.

All of us have a lot to learn about remote learning. We look forward to learning from you and having the opportunity to share your successes.

Points to Ponder

How does this information apply to my current situation?
What are two to three key points to remember?
What is one action step I would like to take?

References

Garmston, R., & Wellman, B. (2013). *The adaptive school: A sourcebook for developing collaborative groups* (2nd ed.). Christopher-Gordon.
International Association for K-12 Online Learning. (2011). *National standards for online teaching.* www.nsqol.org/the-standards/quality-online-teaching
Kotter, J. (2008). *A sense of urgency.* Harvard Business School Publishing.
Kotter, J. (2012). *Leading change.* Harvard Business Review Press.
Williamson, R., & Blackburn, B. (2016). *The principalship from A to Z* (2nd ed.). Routledge.
Williamson, R., & Blackburn, B. (2018). *Rigor in your school: A toolkit for leaders* (2nd ed.). Routledge.
Williamson, R., & Blackburn, B. (2019). *Seven strategies for improving your school.* Routledge.

3

Nurturing Your School's Culture in a Remote Setting

In the last months, schools throughout the United States and the world were required to quickly respond to changing conditions. In an instant, schools were closed and students, teachers and principals were told to work, and learn, remotely. Educators quickly converted instruction from face-to-face to online. In the process, many of the routines of school were abruptly interrupted, changed or even abandoned.

Since then school districts made decisions about how to proceed. Some districts chose to return to face-to-face instruction, and others continued with a totally online remote program. Yet others created a hybrid of the two with a mix of face-to-face and remote learning.

The goal of every district is to return to a traditional face-to-face program. While the future can't be predicted, we anticipate that some form of remote learning will continue for many students, perhaps for inclement-weather days.

The Importance of School Culture

Culture is a rather amorphous concept. It is quite distinct from school climate. While the school's climate reflects the "feeling or tone" of the school, culture reflects the more complex underlying set of values, beliefs and traditions that are present in a school. Culture reveals itself in "the unwritten rules and assumptions, the combination of rituals and traditions, the array of symbols and artifacts, the special language and phrasing that staff and students use, the expectations for change and learning" (Peterson & Deal, 2002, p. 9). Although it looks different, there is a culture in remote learning.

We all know when the culture is positive and good. We also know when it's not good or even toxic. The dilemma is that culture is so subtle that we often don't recognize the things that make it feel "good," "positive" or "supportive."

Culture reflects the often unspoken and unwritten norms about a school. Influential staff members whom others recognize as the informal leaders and opinion makers often transmit it from generation to generation. It's often described as "the way we do things around here" (Bower, 1996).

Ways Leaders Affect Their School's Culture

- What leaders pay attention to, measure and control becomes important.
- The leader's reactions to critical incidents and events.
- Role modeling, teaching and coaching by leaders.
- The criteria for allocation of rewards and status in the school.
- Criteria used for recruiting, selecting and promoting staff.

Adapted from: Schein (2016)

Successful principals recognize the power of culture to shape their school. They are skilled at linking everyday practices in ways that reinforce the core values and mission of their school, whether in a face-to-face or remote setting.

Because a school's culture is reflected in the things that occur every day and in the patterns of behavior and are often so routine that they are simply accepted as "the way we do things around here," it is easy for them to get disrupted in uncertain times like making a transition to remote learning. For example, in a remote learning setting, you have to shift to decisions such as how to balance synchronous and asynchronous learning, the platform(s) used for instruction and how teachers plan together.

What If . . .

I'm a second-year principal, and when I came in, the culture was dysfunctional. I thought we were making progress, but with remote learning, we seem to have taken a step backward. What should I do?

A crisis, or other emergency, like the swift transition to remote learning, destabilizes the best schools. So, I wouldn't be worried. If you were making progress, what you'll want to do is continue to be supportive, to use the same strategies that were working, only adapt them to the remote environment and recognize the stress that goes with any situation that has so much ambiguity and uncertainty.

Indicators of School Culture

A model for understanding school culture was developed and identified several activities that are elements, or indicators, of that culture (Bolman & Deal, 2017).

Indicators of School Culture

Rituals and Ceremonies—These provide structure to our daily life and to the routine of a school. Rituals occur rather routinely, while ceremonies are grander, less frequent events (e.g., graduation). Both rituals and ceremonies reflect values in their structure and their priority and carry meaning about what is valued and what is important.

> *Heroes and Heroines*—Those people who are looked up to as reflecting the organization's values; people who are examples of living the values.
> *Stories and Tales*—Those recollections of events that are told and retold and play a powerful role in sharing examples of organizational values. Stories often contain morals and are inevitably engaging.
> *Rewards and Reinforcements*—These reflect those things that are valued and therefore rewarded. Is it creativity in the classroom or compliance with established patterns? Is it waiving a rule so that a student may be successful or adhering to established policy?
>
> *Adapted from:* Bolman and Deal (2017), Peterson and Deal (2002)

Sustaining Your School's Culture

We're not suggesting a wholesale upending of your school's culture and the adoption of new, unfamiliar routines. Rather, we suggest that you'll want to think about your current norms and how they might be sustained, and even nurtured, in a remote or hybrid environment. Basically, adapt the things you do in a face-to-face environment to meet the needs of a virtual or hybrid model. The familiarity of practices often provides comfort and structure when dealing with change.

As we said earlier, culture is reflected in those patterns of behavior and those norms that are so engrained, they are just the way things are. Those norms reflect strong underlying values and beliefs but emerge as rather routine practices that occur throughout the school year.

Implementation Ideas

Three regularities of school life serve as indicators of your culture. The first is the stories and tales that are told by you, by your teachers and by families who send students to your school.

The second indicator is the ceremonies and rituals that occur throughout the school day and the school year. The third indicator is the recognition of the heroes and heroines among your school community that exemplify your school's values and vision.

Stories and Tales—One way that culture is transmitted is through the power of stories. Much like an oral history, as they are shared from principal to teachers, principal to families or teacher to teacher, they share examples of people or activities that are valued and those you want to continue.

An elementary principal in the state of Washington began planning for the beginning of the next school year last spring. As he remotely interviewed candidates for positions, he asked each person offered a position to make a video that could be shared with new and returning faculty as well as with the families of their students. He asked them to personalize the video but to focus on the sort of things they would say to introduce themselves on opening day. At the same time, the principal is asking his veteran teachers to do something similar. The videos will be shared among the staff and also used to introduce teachers to students and their families.

In Michigan, one middle school principal has accelerated her use of the school's social media sites. The sites have been primarily used to post announcements and share other information. But with the assistance of the school's technology teacher and two students, the principal has begun more frequent sharing of stories about the school, its students and staff and their successes.

In western Michigan, an elementary principal decided to engage more with local online media. That included Patch.com and Nextdoor (nextdoor.com). Both are sites that are focused on regional, or even neighborhood, news. She uses the sites to share short videos or other presentations about the local elementary school. She also says that following both sites serves as an "early warning system" for issues that may be emerging in the local school community.

> **Adopting New Ways to Share Stories**
> - How might you adapt opening day activities to a remote setting?
> - What ways might you use to support and nurture your school community in a remote or hybrid environment?
> - How might you use social media to share stories about teachers, students and successful practices with your community?
> - How can you use your internal platform(s) to share positive stories with other teachers?

Ceremonies and Rituals—Another way that culture is evident is in the routines of school life, the rituals that occur regularly. Similarly, schools have special events and activities throughout the year, and those events, the ceremonies, also are a manifestation of culture.

Daily routines are not often thought of as a reflection of culture, but each one, from balancing synchronous and asynchronous instruction to parent and family communication, reflects values about students, student behavior and school safety.

Ceremonies are those special events that occur during the year. The choice of events and the way they are celebrated signal the school's priorities and values.

In Central Oregon, an elementary school principal talked with Ron about how much she misses the morning routine of greeting students and staff as they arrive, meeting the buses and visiting classrooms to greet students. She said, "The suddenness of moving to remote learning sort of stunned us. Things we used to do routinely, weren't done anymore." But she went on to say that after a few weeks she recognized how important those routines were to everyone, including herself. So, she began to send a short morning greeting to students and staff, sometimes via video, sometimes not. But she always made it upbeat, supportive and encouraging. She kept it short and always thanked people and expressed her appreciation. She also decided to make online visits to classrooms during Zoom lessons. Often she sat quietly and observed. Occasionally she said a few words. "It was important to everyone including the students to know I'm still here."

At an elementary school in Bothell, Washington, the grade-level teams decided that there needed to be a thoughtful plan for their online instruction. So, they adapted the curriculum to fit a new model, one that recognized the constraints some families had accessing technology or due to parent work schedules. Monday and Wednesday were devoted to reading and language arts. Tuesday and Thursday to math and science. Friday was set aside as "social-emotional learning" day, and they worked with their students on team-building activities, including the "Friday themes" they would have had face-to-face. An occasional Friday was pajama day, another stuffed animal day and yet another school colors day. One teacher said, "It added some order to the week for everyone including the teachers. It was just another way of doing what we had done before."

Another example comes from a middle school principal in southeastern Michigan. He described how he missed teachers dropping by the office to talk about issues or even just to chat. So, he began Zoom office hours. He set a time when he would be available online and invited teachers to either schedule an appointment or, perhaps most importantly, just drop by and talk. He was surprised at how many of his teachers dropped by, often just to talk and seek advice. It turned out, he said, "to be one of the most helpful things I did. It was a bit of normal in a very abnormal time."

Adopting New Ways for Routines and Ceremonies
- How might you adapt your beginning or end-of-the-day routines?
- What ways might you continue to be a visible leader in a remote or hybrid environment?

> - How can your school continue with its special activities that occur throughout the school year?
> - How might you use social media to share these activities with students and families?
> - How can you encourage teachers to create and sustain rituals and ceremonies in their classrooms?

Recognizing Heroes and Heroines—A third way that culture is reflected in a school is through the people who are recognized, the heroes and heroines of your school. We often think of formal honors and awards. But it is the subtle, less visible ways that people are honored that can be important. As with the personal stories you tell, the personalization of recognition is essential for students and staff.

We've been talking with teachers and principals around the country about their experience with remote learning. Almost always they talked about the need for support for their work and acknowledgment of everything they've done.

A middle school principal in one of Ron's classes talked about "checking in" with every teacher. "Each week I make sure I include a personal check-in with everyone. It's personal. It's not part of a large Zoom staff meeting. And it's a time I can express my support and ask 'what can I do to support your work?'"

Support can take many forms, and sometimes the most modest recognition can be the most meaningful. One way to celebrate quality instruction is to use "Name It, Claim It and Explain It." In a face-to-face setting, as you see an example of quality instruction in a classroom, take a digital picture or video of what occurs. Then, begin each of your faculty meetings by projecting the picture or video. Explain to your faculty, "I saw something great related to instruction this week. It's up here on the screen. If it belongs to you, stand up and name what you did, claim it as yours, and explain what you were doing."

This is equally effective in a virtual setting. Take a screenshot or edit a portion of a video from a teacher's lesson. You could post it on a platform such as Flipgrid or share via email. After the appropriate teacher claims and explains it, other teachers can respond.

Most teachers and principals are grappling with the change to remote learning. By being patient, compassionate and sensitive with teachers, leaders can model the ways we want them to interact with students and families.

One elementary school principal in North Carolina talked with Ron about the importance of finding resources for teachers. "They need both instructional support as well as technical support. My job is to make that available." She described how she designed a weekly professional development newsletter with links to online resources, stories about the work of other teachers across the country and different ideas for supporting students and families.

At one middle school in southern Michigan, the principal described how her teachers began to accumulate examples of funny things that occurred online. They included everything from student snacks while online to the things students wanted to show the rest of the class. One student used his tablet to conduct an online tour of his home but forgot to clear it with the rest of their family. The examples also included funny things teachers had done. One teacher actually conducted class from her walk-in closet, the only place she could get away from other family members who were also online or working from home.

Every week, the principal collected the examples, and the staff voted on the "example of the week." Much like the TV show *America's Funniest Home Videos*, this award served as a way to have a little fun and acknowledge the trials and tribulations of the move to remote learning.

Adopting New Ways for Recognition

- How might you adapt the way you recognize students and staff for the remote setting?
- What recognition could you create for use in a remote or hybrid environment?
- How will you use remote learning tools to recognize families and parents?

Sustaining Your Culture

One way to begin planning for sustaining your culture is to assess the areas we discussed and determine how you would adapt them to a totally remote or hybrid learning setting. It's most helpful if you identify specific practices using the guiding questions, then modify them as appropriate.

	Guiding Questions	How to Apply in a Remote Setting
Rituals and Ceremonies	♦ What are the routines and rituals in your school? What values do they represent? ♦ Are there special ceremonies or events at your school? What do they celebrate? ♦ What messages do you communicate in your daily actions, classroom visits and other interactions with members of your school community?	
Heroes and Heroines	♦ Who are the heroes or heroines on your staff? Why are they recognized? How do you provide that recognition? ♦ What ways do you identify and celebrate people who contribute to the success of your school?	
Stories and Tales	♦ How do you communicate verbally and through your actions with your faculty and staff? What underlying messages are represented? ♦ What are the stories you tell about your school, its students and staff? What stories do you encourage others to tell?	

Launching a New School Year in a Remote Setting

The beginning of the school year is an important ritual, one filled with all sorts of messages about your school's values and its mission. As many school districts moved to a remote or hybrid learning model, they grappled with how to launch the school year in a way that was reassuring for students and their families, as well as teachers and other staff. A major part of that reassurance manifested itself in continuing many of the routines from previous school years.

There continues to be great uncertainty about the look of the current school year. Will schools provide face-to-face instruction? Or will schools open as virtual programs or hybrids of the two? Will face-to-face instruction return mid-year? Will families choose to send their children back to school if the program is face-to-face? Or will families select virtual options?

Despite the uncertainty, it's critical that every school year get off to a good start. Teachers and principals don't want to add to the uncertainty or to the stress of students and families. Here are three areas where we suggest extra attention for these uncertain times.

The Bottom Line Is Safety

As the start of the school year looms, safety has become the most important issue for teachers, other employees, families and students. It's both physical safety and social-emotional safety. Whether in a traditional or remote setting, there are a variety of reasons people may feel unsafe.

Reasons Faculty, Staff or Students May Feel Unsafe

Medical issues (personal and family).
Family job changes or job loss.
Family financial issues.
Family member(s) separation or death.
Housing instability or homelessness.
Food insecurity.

It's important to remember that both employees and students and their families have been affected by the pandemic in ways you may not know. Have friends or loved ones become ill?

Have family members' job status changed? Have extended family members joined the household? Do employees, or their loved ones, have pre-existing medical conditions that make them more vulnerable?

Feeling safe is a complex physiological reaction to events and the environment. But the Mayo Clinic and other health care providers offer some tips to help you think about navigating the anxiety associated with launching a new school year while in a remote setting (Hubbard, 2020; Markham, 2020).

- **Acknowledge the Anxiety**—When talking with people, acknowledge the anxiety that is present. Describe safety protocols, but don't get defensive. It's best to provide safety procedures in writing so people can refer to them at a later time. Willingly answer every question, and offer to speak with anyone individually if they prefer. Understand that everyone has a different level of comfort or concern about dealing with the crisis.
- **Establish New Routines**—Routine and structure provide calm and help reduce anxiety. Don't talk in generalities about safety, but instead offer specific plans about your school's new routines for things like lunch, entry and exit from the building or changing classes.
- **Look for and Share the Good**—As you talk with teachers and with families and students, look for good things that are happening. Identify positive activities or trends. Share those things to help people become more hopeful and focus on problem-solving.
- **Encourage Self-Care**—Talk with teachers and other employees about the importance of caring for themselves. Encourage them to take time every day for themselves and doing things that contribute to their own well-being.
- **Reach Out**—A connection to others contributes to feeling safe and reduces anxiety. Make time every day to personally connect with teachers and other employees. Talk with them. Ask for their feedback. Seek their opinion. Listen. Do the same for students and families.

- **Extend Grace**—This school year will not be normal. Give yourself as well as your teachers, students and families some extra grace. Forgive the brash comment. Don't react to the forgotten deadline. Be flexible when you can.

Communicate Often and Disseminate Broadly

During this crisis there's a lot of misinformation shared through social media and other sources. It's important that your school become hypervigilant about monitoring what's being shared about your school and its plans. It's essential that you become even more transparent about your own plans and preparations. In the absence of information, people tend to form their own opinions, and often share those, even when they're inaccurate.

There are several tips for sharing information about the start of a new school year.

- **Communicate Often**—Frequent updates to families and students let them know you're planning for the new year and build confidence in you as a reliable source of information.
- **Disseminate Broadly**—Don't rely on a single method for communicating. You can utilize traditional formats like newsletters but be sure to post them on your school's website. Take advantage of social media (Facebook, Twitter, Instagram) to share information as well. Monitor those sites to identify questions or concerns that may emerge. Be prepared to address rumors that stakeholders may have heard or seen.
- **Be Transparent and Unfailingly Honest**—Never mislead. If you don't have an answer, say so, and commit to getting the answer. During a crisis people want assurance that the information they receive is trustworthy.
- **Listen as Well as Share**—Use your communication tools and social media to authentically listen to what families and students are saying. This can help identify issues that are bubbling up and allow you to monitor the current

tenor of your school community. You'll also want to be regularly available to teachers, staff, families and other stakeholders.

Sustain the Routines

There's comfort in the patterns and routines of daily life in a school. Those activities provide a structure that helps to organize and sustain a school. In times of uncertainty, it can be even more important to maintain those patterns of behavior. If your school is offering a face-to-face program, continue those routines but appropriately adapt them to new safety protocols. If your school is a virtual or hybrid model, adapt the routines to fit your new model.

Here are some ways you can sustain your school's culture during the current crisis.

- **Adapt Daily Routines**—Think about the daily school routines like greeting students in the morning, taking attendance, lunch or the end of the day. Rather than abandon some routines because of concerns about social distancing or other safety concerns, adapt them to the new environment. A Michigan middle school principal, a fan of videos on TikTok, decided to create a weekly video incorporating music and movement to greet students and staff, promote school spirit and make important announcements for the week. Other administrators, teachers and staff often join him. It's emailed to all students and staff early Monday morning and has become an important way to launch each week of remote learning. It's become one of the school's "new" rituals.
- **Share the Stories**—Stories are powerful. They are the oral history that can be shared from person to person and often define the culture of a school. As you talk with your teachers, students and families, listen for their stories, the things they're doing or the activities they're involved in that reflect your school's values and support its mission. Then share those with others in your school community.

- **Check In With Your Teachers**—In these uncertain times it is essential that you talk with your teachers, learn about their work, discuss the challenges they face and identify ways you can support them. One middle school principal in Michigan whose school was also virtual talked with Ron about "checking in" with every teacher every few days. Rather than joining a large Zoom meeting, he provided an individual, personal time to simply talk with each teacher. He reported that most of the time "I was just listening" but "it was important for them to know I was there, that I cared, and that I really wanted to support their work."

Final Thoughts

While great uncertainty remains about the structure of the school year, it's important for leaders to recognize the need to support and care for the members of their school community. It's important to recognize the power of culture. Often, it is the patterns and routines that are reflective of a school's culture that sustain students, teachers and families in times of adversity and challenge.

Points to Ponder

How does this information apply to my current situation?
What are two to three key points to remember?
What is one action step I would like to take?

References

Blackburn, B. (2020). *Rigor in the remote learning classroom: Instructional tips and strategies*. Routledge.

Bolman, L., & Deal, T. E. (2017). *Reframing organizations: Artistry, choice and leadership* (6th ed.). John Wiley & Sons, Inc.

Bower, M. (1996). *Will to manage*. McGraw Hill.

Hubbard, L. (2020). 9 ways to tame anxiety during the COVID-19 pandemic. *Mayo Clinic.* www.mayoclinichealthsystem.org/hometown-health/speaking-of-health/9-ways-to-tame-anxiety-during-the-covid-19-pandemic

Markham, L. (2020). Coping with fear in the face of a pandemic. *Psychology Today.* www.psychologytoday.com/us/blog/peaceful-parents-happy-kids/202003/coping-fear-in-the-face-pandemic

Peterson, K. D., & Deal, T. E. (2002). *The shaping school culture fieldbook.* Jossey-Bass.

Schein, E. (2016). *Organizational culture and leadership* (5th ed.). Jossey-Bass.

Williamson, R., & Blackburn, B. (2016). *The principalship from A to Z* (2nd ed.). Routledge.

Williamson, R., & Blackburn, B. (2018). *Rigor in your school: A toolkit for leaders* (2nd ed.). Routledge.

Williamson, R., & Blackburn, B. (2019). *Seven strategies for improving your school.* Routledge.

4

Maintaining a Collaborative Remote Learning School

Collaboration is critical to the success of any school, especially one that is using remote learning. The evidence indicates that decisions are better, have greater support and are more likely to be implemented if they are the result of intentional collaboration with teachers, staff and parents.

The days of a solitary leader disappeared decades ago. But leaders still struggle with how to involve others in decision-making and how to build a viable and successful shared decision-making model. In every school you can find examples of involvement in decision-making. Sometimes it is systematic, intentional and deals with vital curricular and instructional issues. Other times it's simply a way for the principal to ask about managerial concerns.

There is no formula or perfect method for collaborative decision-making; however, it is most successful when the involvement is authentic, timely and a routine part of the school's operations.

> **Examples of Teacher Involvement in Decision-Making**
>
> **Professional Development Committee:** Teachers on the committee review applications from teachers for online conferences and make recommendations and decisions about needed professional development for the school, such as providing scaffolding during remote learning.
>
> **School Improvement Committee:** Teachers and parents work with the principal to set school priorities, determine student equity actions and allocate technology resources.
>
> **Principal's Advisory Committee:** This group provides the principal with advice about important decisions, including the format and scheduling of remote learning. They serve as a sounding board for both day-to-day routines and important policy changes.
>
> **Budget Review Committee:** Some principals share information about the school's budget with teachers and work with a small group to make decisions about spending priorities.

Benefits and Challenges

There are many benefits of shared decision-making:

- Higher-quality decisions because more perspectives are considered
- Increased job satisfaction and morale
- Heightened sense of empowerment
- Greater ownership of school goals and priorities when participants have a stake in the decision
- Improved student achievement because of greater coordination of work among teachers

On the other hand, there are also challenges or potential obstacles to shared decision-making, which include the following:

- Expanded participation may require more time to make decisions

- Group dynamics may stifle ideas, leading to "groupthink"
- Polarization around specific points of view
- People feeling left out or that some have greater access and opportunity to influence decisions

Involving others may require more time for planning, time for discussion and analysis of alternatives. But the payoff is better decisions, decisions that have considered alternatives and decisions that have greater support among stakeholders.

What If . . .

I understand the benefits of shared decision-making, but my teachers are so overwhelmed with remote learning, they don't want anything else to do.

The transition to remote learning has required a lot from teachers. Acknowledge and thank your teachers for everything they've done. You probably already have some shared decision-making structures like a school improvement team. Continue to use them. You can also involve people by doing a quick online poll about an issue, by talking one-on-one with key teacher leaders and gauging their opinion or by asking for volunteers.

Ensure Positive Dynamics Among School Personnel

It is important that you nurture and sustain a collaborative culture, one that embraces open, honest conversation about remote learning. You may discover some part of the transition plan needs additional attention or that additional professional development will be helpful.

That's normal. You need to resist the tendency to point fingers, to blame other people or to blame factors outside of your school. We don't ever believe that is helpful. The power to monitor implementation and adjust plans lies within the school with teachers and administrators.

We've worked with hundreds of schools in every region of the United States and identified behaviors that can be harmful to your success. Similarly, we've identified behaviors that can support your culture of collaboration and your remote learning plan.

Inhibitors	Facilitators
People are reluctant to share data about things that aren't working.	People are comfortable sharing data about what doesn't work. They are not penalized for doing so.
People use opinions, rather than data, to support their positions.	People support their suggestions with data, facts and solid logic.
People agree to a decision, yet do little to support its success.	People support mutually agreed-upon decisions and work to make the decision succeed.
People seek personal credit for success.	People credit others for success.
People disagree to improve their own interests rather than to find the best answer.	People are comfortable disagreeing and focused on finding the best response to the current issue.
People find blame, seeking culprits rather than identifying causes.	People analyze experiences to identify ways to improve.
People blame people or conditions outside of the school for lack of success.	People accept full responsibility for successes as well as failures.
The leader avoids critical input and does not ask questions to clarify thinking.	The leader asks lots of questions, challenges thinking and values discussion and critical insight into issues.

Adapted from: Collins (2009)

You may recognize some of these behaviors, both positive and negative. That's the thing about groups: they tend to generate strong emotions, especially if it's an issue that people care deeply about. When circumstances, like moving to remote learning, occur unexpectedly, the dynamic will change. Your job as a leader is to recognize what is happening and help your team restore balance in their work and decision-making.

The dynamics of groups can be an issue but one that can also be addressed. The most successful collaborative groups develop their own norms for how the group will function and how they will make a decision. In addition to a decision-making model, they often include things like how to involve everyone in the discussion, how to avoid distractions and how to record and share decisions that were made. Barbara uses a standard set of norms when working with teachers.

Sample Norms for Discourse

- We are all a team, so we work together rather than competing.
- We respect each other and act appropriately.
- We actively listen to each other, which allows us to authentically contribute our perspectives.
- If you don't agree with someone, find a positive way to respond without embarrassing the other person.
- Everyone should be able to participate. If one person is talking too much, the other group members should give them a signal and move on.
- The process is just as important as the result. We want to think deeply about our work, elaborate, justify our points and pose additional questions to promote more thinking.
- Making mistakes is normal; it helps us learn.
- If you need help, check out the online Resource Board or Frequently Asked Questions.

A related issue is polarization that can occur around specific points of view. Successful groups welcome diverse perspectives but recognize the importance of establishing norms around discussion, use of data or expertise and entrenched points of view. One middle school principal in suburban Phoenix established a norm that when speaking to an issue, you could not cite your own "experience." Individuals needed to cite research or guidance from a professional organization. That limited the use of phrases like "in my 30 years I've found . . .".

Finally, people who feel left out or believe that others have greater access and opportunity to influence decisions can create tension. An inclusive group that represents all factions of a school community is critical. We'll provide more information about handling conflict later in this chapter.

Overall, the long-term benefits of collaborative decision-making outweigh the short-term obstacles. When teachers, staff and families are active partners in decisions about their school, they have more ownership of the school's direction and a greater commitment to its success.

Planning for Shared Decision-Making

It's important to decide whom to involve. Ask yourself two questions:

1. Who is most closely involved?
2. How much can people contribute? What is their level of expertise?

You might also consider other factors in order to facilitate your decision. Hoy and Tarter (2008) suggested that if people have a stake in the outcome and have some level of expertise, they should be involved. If people are indifferent to the outcome and have no expertise, no involvement is needed. Finally, if people are concerned with the outcome but lack expertise or have expertise but are indifferent, then they should have limited participation.

Things to Consider
- What is the task?
- Who has a stake in the decision?
- Who should appropriately be involved because of their expertise or their role?

- How will the group be organized?
- What are the group norms?
- How will the decision be made?
- What is the timeline for completion of the task?

Your school improvement team will continue its work during remote learning, but you may also want to consider task-specific teams like a transition team, a virtual instruction team, an equity team and a parent and family communication team. Expanding participation provides more perspectives on the issues, broadens ownership of your plan and contributes to greater employee satisfaction.

Transition Team

Transition teams assist in planning transitions, whether that is to remote learning, to or from hybrid instruction or with on-site instruction. Schools are in varying stages of transitions, and transitions may be ongoing due to health crises, natural disasters or other issues. Detail-oriented stakeholders can provide an essential service on this team. There are a variety of concerns the team may explore.

Transition Concerns

Scheduling.
Access to appropriate resources for students.
Access to appropriate resources for teachers.
Access to needed Internet and/or Internet speed.
Communication for all stakeholders.

Virtual Instruction Team

Next, it's important to have a group that is focused on instruction in the virtual setting. Although transitional issues are more urgent, instructional issues are likely more important. Many of these issues may be addressed at the district level to provide a more uniform experience for families. For this team, you will want your strongest instructional leaders.

Virtual Instruction Concerns

What platform(s) or app(s) will we use?

How will we provide adequate training so teachers are comfortable with remote instruction?

How will we provide instruction on navigating the platform(s) to students and parents?

How does our instruction ensure appropriate scaffolding for students who need it?

How does our instruction provide for ongoing assessment so we can meet students' needs?

How will we ensure rigor for all students?

Equity Team

The role of an equity team is to ensure that the needs of every single student are met, no matter the situation. For this team, we would include teachers of specialized groups as well as any teachers who are particularly passionate about equity. Responding to equity issues is discussed in Chapters 8 and 9.

Equity Concerns

How do we ensure students have appropriate technology and Internet access?

How do we ensure appropriate instruction for special groups of students, such as students with special needs, English learners or gifted students?

> How do we ensure appropriate support to parents and families, especially those with vulnerable students?
> How are we accommodating students for whom synchronous learning is an issue?
> How are we addressing social-emotional issues?

Parent and Family Communication Team

Finally, a parent and family communication team can focus on this crucial area that will provide support for other teams. In addition to teachers, you may want to include parents and family members for a different perspective. If possible, include a family member from a more vulnerable situation to share an essential viewpoint.

> ### Parent and Family Communication Concerns
> How can we regularly communicate with every parent and family, even those with limited electronic avenues?
> How can we scaffold instruction for parents and families (providing schedules, tip sheets, etc.)?
> How can we understand and meet the diverse needs of parents and families?
> How can we provide parent and family training on different topics?

Ultimately, decide which teams you need based on the unique needs of your school. Also, be really clear about tasks so that you avoid miscommunication and conflicting recommendations and plans. You may want to use your current school improvement team as the group that receives recommendations and resolves any conflicts.

Checklist for Formation of Teams

_____ Is the purpose clear? Is the role well defined?
_____ Is the team needed to address an important issue?
_____ Is membership representative? Is membership appropriate to the task?
_____ Do we have an appropriate format for meeting, both electronic and face-to-face?
_____ Are there agreed-upon norms for operation? For decision-making?
_____ Is there a mechanism to communicate with the larger school community? With other decision-making groups?
_____ What is the process for concluding the team's work?

The bottom line is to be sure the purpose of each team is clear and the roles are well defined and understood.

What If . . .

I have a long-time teacher who is active in our teams simply due to the length of her teaching career. However, she is not a productive member of any of our teams. In fact, she can be destructive to our process. How do I deal with this?

> *There's nothing wrong with talking with that teacher about her behavior, particularly since you describe it as destructive. Be sure to have specific examples of the way she behaved. Some people behave differently once they're made aware that others recognize what they're doing. Be prepared for a negative reaction. Remember, your job is to advocate for the good of your school and for your entire instructional team. One structural suggestion is to have term limits. Some schools clearly limit the*

length of time someone can serve. Others designate roles or grade levels that can be part of the decision-making team. They do this to expand the voices and points of view on committees.

Structures to Support Effective Collaboration in a Remote Setting

As we look at a variety of strategies for collaborating in the remote learning setting, we'll start with the foundations of effective collaboration. Let's look at three: the right tools, the right space and team building.

The Right Tools

First, you'll want to have the right tools in place for your teachers and other stakeholders. You'll want tools that provide opportunities that match your goals and purposes. For example, if you want teachers to work together to assess student work, a platform that allows for document sharing is critical.

Goal or Purpose	Sample Platform
Group discussion	Synchronous video program such as Microsoft Teams, Google Hangouts or Zoom audio conference call
Group discussion (lower Internet speeds)	Platform with chat or messaging function such as Google Hangouts, Microsoft Teams or Slack
Create, analyze or revise work samples	Shared document programs such as Dropbox, Google Docs or Microsoft One Drive
Comprehensive program for collaboration	Platforms such as Canvas, Blackboard or Google Suite

The Right Space

It may sound odd to talk about space for collaboration, but it is important. When we are in the school building, we are able to work together in the classroom in a small group, or perhaps the library for a full faculty meeting. We may post key information near mailboxes, and we may have a common room for resources. We need similar spaces online in order to work collaboratively.

First, it's important to have a place to gather as a grade level, team or department. Many teachers use a video chat platform to meet at a specified time, but you may want to have these smaller groups work together during a large group faculty meeting or professional development. Most platforms, such as Zoom, allow for breakout rooms, which can be quite effective. In a recent series of professional development sessions, Barbara was able to introduce a strategy and then organize breakout sessions by subject area so teachers could apply it for their purposes. If your teachers want to collaborate on assignments or assessments, they will need their own folders for shared documents, which may need to be individual or for small groups.

Next, teachers will need a place to organize ongoing information. This will include shared resources, key information, newsletters or answers to frequently asked questions. It is also beneficial to have a place to share updates, such as describing successes to celebrate. Facebook groups are a viable option to meet this need.

Finally, you'll want to ensure that teachers have options for communicating with other individuals or small groups. These can include private messages, email or direct messages on a platform such as Twitter. Also, most synchronous video platforms provide the opportunity for private chat.

Team Building

Finally, we want to consider the concept of team building. In an article on effective collaboration while working remotely, Dhawan and Chamorro-Premuzic (2018) describe three kinds of distance when collaborating remotely.

Type of Distance	*Explanation*
Physical	Place and time
Operational	Team size, bandwidth and skill levels
Affinity	Values, trust and interdependency

They point out the best way to improve team performance is to reduce affinity distance, since you have few options for affecting the other factors. For example, you can use video calls, rather than voice calls, because being able to see one another increases closeness, contributing to trust.

There are other ways to build team collaboration using positive rituals. For example, one school we talked uses "Tuesday Treats." Faculty gather virtually at the end of the school day, with each person bringing their own "treats." After teachers informally share their treat and promise recipes to those who want them, they share successes related to their students. These types of activities can enhance your collaborative efforts.

Collaborative Team Members

In order to have a collaborative school environment, you must have faculty, staff and other stakeholders who value working in a collaborative manner. There are six key characteristics of a collaborative team member.

Characteristics of a Collaborative Team Member
Weighs personal and group goals.
Focuses on student learning.
Shows genuine curiosity.
Respects group members' strengths.
Balances speaking and listening.
Handles conflict constructively.

Balances Goals

First, a team member who is collaborative is able to balance their personal and group goals. In other words, they are able to weigh the importance of their own goals and the group's goals and find a way to achieve both and resolve any conflict. For example, if a teacher wants to improve parent and family communication but the overall school goal is to improve student learning, he or she can reframe the goals. From a new perspective, we can address ways to improve student learning, with one particular strategy incorporating family communication and collaboration.

Focuses on Student Learning

An effective collaborator also focuses on student learning. We just discussed the importance of stakeholders balancing personal and group goals. Unfortunately, it is very easy to become distracted by personal agendas. All too frequently we've heard issues portrayed as affecting students when in fact it was an issue affecting an individual teacher or group of teachers.

At a recent workshop about developing a remediation plan for at-risk students, two teachers began to argue about technology and their own scheduling needs. The two continued to bicker for some time until the principal reminded everyone that the purpose of the remediation classes was to positively affect student learning for their neediest students. By reframing the conversation to a focus on student learning, the group was able to move forward.

Shows Curiosity

Next, a skilled collaborator shows genuine curiosity. Rather than being a passive participant during collaborative work, these colleagues are eager to learn. They ask questions, probe for more information and share their own ideas when appropriate.

Sample Questions That Reflect Curiosity

Have you seen that idea used in a classroom? What did you think?

Have you used it in your own classroom? How did it work?

Where did you hear about the idea? How can I learn more?

Why do you think this would work in a remote learning setting?

What adaptations do you think would help us improve student learning? Why?

Respects Strengths

Closely tied to the skill of curiosity is that a good collaborator respects the strengths of others in the group. Unfortunately, there are times in education that an atmosphere of competition, particularly regarding standardized test scores or ratings, overshadows any collaborative work. In that case, leaders must work to shift the overall atmosphere from competition to cooperation. One facet of that process is the ability of team members to respect each other. Opportunities to identify and reinforce strengths of other group members should be a regular part of the collaborative process. A true collaborator not only recognizes the strengths of others, he or she validates those strengths and encourages others to do the same.

Personality Characteristic	*Value for Collaboration*
Cautious	Ensures we look at all possibilities rather than rushing into a decision
Action-oriented	Ensures a final decision will be made
Creative	Ensures we "think out of the box" and look at a variety of options
Friendly	Helps smooth over conflicts and facilitate teamwork
Straightforward	Cuts through the clutter and "noise" to get to the main point(s)

Speaking and Listening

Next, a stakeholder who collaborates well with others balances how much they speak and how much they listen. We've all been in groups where one person dominates a conversation. You might think this does not happen as often in a virtual setting, but it can. We've seen teachers take over a Zoom meeting, dominate a chat or overwhelm a shared document platform with information. Barbara once saw a sign: *Nature gave us two ears and one mouth so we could listen twice as much as we speak.* That's not a bad guide. Skilled collaborators share information but listen to be sure they are contributing in a positive way.

> **How to Listen Online**
>
> Look at the speaker when in a synchronous session, even when they are not looking at you.
> Be attentive to the conversation rather than multitasking.
> Ask questions to clarify what you have heard.
> Take notes or create a mind map to connect ideas.
> Help everyone stay on task; if chats are discussing a different topic, redirect or suggest holding this information to a later time.

Handles Conflict

Although there can be conflict in any collaborative work, it can be intensified in virtual settings. Because team members are not able to see nonverbal cues, they can take the comments as ones that are more personal than normal. For example, if a teacher comments in a chat that he "thinks we all just need to pay attention to our struggling students," in a face-to-face setting, other teachers may realize he is expressing frustration. However, because teachers are looking at words on a page, it may appear as if he is blaming other teachers and stating that some teachers are not doing their jobs. It's also easier for conflict to escalate, as people are likely to quickly respond without reflecting on their comments. I'm sure you have seen evidence of this, perhaps in comments on an online news article or on Facebook.

There are several ways to minimize conflict and handle it appropriately, most of which should be modeled and organized by the leader. First, whenever possible, use live video chats, which are the next best things to on-site, face-to-face meetings. When using video chats, ask members to turn on their videos, so all participants can see faces. Next, allocate time to focus on the strengths each person brings to the group. "Cheers for Peers" allow group members to celebrate positive actions or characteristics of others. You might also use this strategy is a chat prior to a video conference. Beginning with positive examples sets the tone for the meeting. Finally, provide a nondistracting method for sharing complaints. You might use an electronic version of the feedback form provided here. Ask teachers and stakeholders to make notes on the form, reflect on the form after the meeting for a set period of time (such as one hour) and then send it to you for discussion or needed actions.

Frustration Form	
I'm frustrated about . . .	
Here's what I would like to talk about or here's what I think we should do . . .	
Post-Discussion Recommendations _____ Discuss concern with other person (instructional coach, grade level, team or department chair, other teachers) _____ Take action within own classroom _____ Realize we can't do anything about it right now, but we can consider it later _____ Recognize this issue is a mandate or part of a bigger picture and will not change	

Assessing Strengths and Challenges

As you are working with your teachers and other stakeholders to develop their collaboration skills, consider each desired characteristic and note the strengths and challenges of each group member, which will allow you and other leaders to facilitate positive collaboration.

Teacher or Other Stakeholder:		
Characteristic	*Strengths*	*Challenges*
Weighs personal and group goals		
Focuses on student learning as the ultimate result		
Shows genuine curiosity		
Respects group members' strengths		

(Continued)

Teacher or Other Stakeholder:		
Characteristic	Strengths	Challenges
Balances speaking and listening		
Handles conflict in a constructive manner		

Assessing Collaborative Efforts

Finally, you will want to assess collaborative efforts. Assessments allow you to make short-term and long-term adjustments, as well as measuring the success of your group(s). We recommend using a two-part process. First, based on standard criteria, each group member assesses whether the team reached the goal, is making progress or needs work. They should write an example or justification of their choices. Next, provide an open-ended portion so they can provide any other input.

Assessment of Collaborative Efforts			
Criteria	Reached the Goal	Making Progress	We Need Work
Members exhibit true collaborative behaviors			
Membership represents the diversity of the community			
Group works toward clear purpose			
Recommendations are geared toward school's goals and will positively affect student learning			
All members provided appropriate input into decision-making			
Team members felt supported by school leadership			

Assessment of Collaborative Efforts			
Criteria	Reached the Goal	Making Progress	We Need Work
I thought the best aspects were . . .			
I thought the area(s) that needed improvement was/were . . .			
I'd also like you to know . . .			

A Final Note

Collaboration can improve decisions, empower teachers and other stakeholders and develop ownership for long-term improvement. By choosing and developing the right teams that meet your needs, providing the right structures for collaborations and developing the collaborative skills of team members, you will see a variety of benefits to your school.

Points to Ponder

How does this information apply to my current situation?
What are two to three key points to remember?
What is one action step I would like to take?

References

Blackburn, B. (2020). *Rigor in the remote learning classroom: Instructional tips and strategies*. Routledge.

Blackburn, R., Blackburn, B., & Williamson, R. (2018). *Advocacy from A to Z*. Routledge.

Collins, J. (2009). *How the mighty fall*. Harper Collins.

Dhawan, E., & Chamorro-Premuzic, T. (2018). *How to collaborate effectively if your team is remote*. https://hbr.org/2018/02/how-to-collaborate-effectively-if-your-team-is-remote

Hoy, W., & Tarter, C. (2008). *Administrators solving the problems of practice: Decision-making concepts, cases and consequences* (3rd ed.). Pearson Education.

Williamson, R., & Blackburn, B. (2016). *The principalship from A to Z* (2nd ed.). Routledge.

Williamson, R., & Blackburn, B. (2018). *Rigor in your school: A toolkit for leaders* (2nd ed.). Routledge.

Williamson, R., & Blackburn, B. (2019). *Seven strategies for improving your school*. Routledge.

5

Communicating Effectively During Remote Learning

One of the most important skills for a school leader is communication. Everything you do uses some form of communication, whether face-to-face, online, via email or on social media.

If you can't communicate effectively, your message will never be heard.

How Can I Be Effective?

There are specific ways to improve your communication. First, let's look at ten general principles of effective communication. Then, we'll turn our attention to specific tips for online communication.

Ten Principles of Effective Communication

Conciseness and consistency matter.
Open with your key point.
Match to your agenda.

> Make it coherent.
> Understand your audience.
> Name your objective/desired action.
> Courtesy rules.
> Ask questions.
> Tell a story.
> Empathy helps.

Conciseness and Consistency Matter

It's important to have a concise message, whether verbal or written. Oftentimes, your listeners are busy and they do not have a tremendous amount of time to give you. If you take too much time, they will either move on or tune out. Additionally, be consistent in your message. If you send unclear messages that are not consistent, you will confuse your audience.

Open With Your Key Point

We live in a busy world and your audience will be busy. Start your verbal or written message with your key point. Begin with the most important thing you have to say. This way, if your listener does interrupt you or tunes you out, you will still have communicated your main point.

Match to Your Agenda

Next, be sure your message matches your agenda. You may be thinking this is common sense, but you might be surprised how often this does not occur. For example, we heard one principal discuss safety in a hybrid model. Her goal was to convince the superintendent and cabinet to provide overtime expenses so custodians could complete a deep cleaning every afternoon. But in her one-page fact sheet, she never stated that as her goal. Instead, she simply shared information about the importance of school cleanliness without focusing on her agenda. The decision makers were left with information but without a clear idea of what the principal wanted.

Make It Coherent

Similarly, you want to have a coherent message. If you stray off topic, you will lose your audience. Unfortunately, it's too easy to do this. A lack of focus can undermine your advocacy efforts. Know your point and stick to it.

Understand Your Audience

As you craft your message, you'll want to understand your audience. As you interact with different stakeholders, you will find that each person has different needs, goals and prior experiences related to your agenda. Once you discover where they are coming from, you can tailor your message to them, and your chances of being effective are improved.

Name Your Objective/Desired Action

As you are delivering your message, be sure to ask for help with your objective or ask for a specific action. If we only present material, the stakeholder is left with information but no idea what they're being asked to do. That's nice, but what do you want them to do with that information?

Issue	*Desired Objective/Action*
Equitable remote instruction	Additional funding for laptop computers and wireless service
Rigor throughout online instruction	Provide funding for online professional development and stipends for teachers to collaborate to adapt assignments and assessments
Smaller class size, which will allow for hybrid instruction	Options such as use of gymnasium, cafeteria or other indoor spaces; use of outdoor space if possible; possible additional teachers or support staff

Courtesy Rules

As you communicate with stakeholders and influencers, courtesy should be at the forefront. We don't always see courtesy used in the advocacy process, but if you want to accomplish your goals, you will make more progress if you are considerate. This includes our words but also our nonverbal communication.

Nonverbal communication is particularly important. The wordless symbols we send can reinforce or negate our communication. Nonverbal signals can be positive if used correctly, or they can send a message that contradicts our advocacy efforts. Types of nonverbal communication include facial expressions, body movements and posture, gestures, touch, eye contact, space and voice. This is a particularly important consideration with online interactions, since the other person(s) may not be able to read these signals. Online, adapt your video presence and written communication, knowing you don't have the full range of nonverbal cues to support your message.

Ask Questions

Another important concept is to ask questions while you are delivering your message. People are more responsive when you talk with them, not at them. Part of effectively asking questions is listening. You should listen just as much as you talk. Asking questions is one way to have a conversation, rather than simply stating information. The use of open-ended inquiry questions promotes dialogue.

Tell a Story

As you are sharing information, tell a story that supports your ideas. Stories are personal, and people remember stories longer than they remember facts. If possible, you want to tell a firsthand account of a story, something that happened to you or that you experienced. However, secondhand stories can also be effective. Perhaps you can explain a personal experience someone else shared with you, such as how this issue will affect a child in your school. The point is: stories are effective, particularly if they tug at the heartstrings.

Empathy Helps

Finally, be empathetic with your audience. By showing that you understand where they are coming from, they will be more likely to listen to you. For example, you may be advocating for more money for career/technical education. You might want to speak with local business leaders or business groups like the chamber of commerce. Be sensitive to the local tax rate but at the same time stress how good career/technical education programs can provide skilled workers and lower training costs for new employees. In other words, turn it into a win-win for both business owners and the schools.

Effective Online Communication

You'll want to incorporate the ten principles we have just discussed when communicating online. It is a given that you do not want to share any inappropriate content; however, whether you are using email, social media or online video, there are some additional considerations.

Effective Online Communication

Be respectful.
Share with discretion.
Double-check your posts.

Be Respectful

We know the importance of being respectful when communicating. In an online setting, there are several specific tips regarding respect. First, it's okay to take a breath before responding to an email or social media post. Online communication lends itself to speed, and sometimes we say something that we later regret. Also consider that sarcasm doesn't translate well online. Our listener or reader can't see us, so there is no body language to soften our comments. On a more basic level, don't use all caps. When you do, that is interpreted as shouting.

Earlier, we talked about the importance of listening, but it is worth revisiting here. In a video chat, if you talk too much, the other person(s) does not have a chance to speak. The software may not have a tool for raising your hand, or other participants become tired of trying to jump into the conversation. In a written format, such as social media posting, I have learned that if you are constantly posting and replying to every single comment, that can translate into shouting over other people. A good rule of thumb is to match the tone and length of other people in online conversations, postings or chats.

Share With Discretion

Next, it's important to share information, pictures, video and comments with discretion. In other words, think before you share! What are some specific examples of discretionary sharing? First, respect the privacy of others. For example, don't forward an email unless you have permission from the original sender. Second, don't share in a way that excludes people. Working with a group of teachers, Barbara saw a posting that was clearly directed at one person in the group, but it was posted for the entire group. It also included sensitive information that led several group members to feel excluded. In that case, a direct message would have been more discreet.

Double-Check Your Posts

Finally, always double-check your social media postings or re-read your emails. We were reminded of the importance of this from a principal. She was sent information related to resources available in the town for students and families in need. Without thinking, she forwarded it to all teachers so they could share it with students and families. One of her teachers quickly responded, informing the principal that one of the groups referenced was no longer in business and one was under investigation for criminal activities.

Another principal received information about purchasing hand sanitizer at a reduced price, which he did. He later discovered it contained an unsafe ingredient and was not recommended by the government. Both of these are strong reminders to fact-check information.

It's also important to protect personal information for teachers and students. This does not mean you are unable to share news from your school; just be careful. Your district likely has a policy regarding using photos of students, and it may require parental permission. If there is not a policy, that is still good practice. However, we sometimes do not consider protecting our teachers, which is also important. Barbara taught a graduate student who was a middle school teacher. She came to class one night very upset. She was named teacher of the year, and her principal shared the information across all his social media channels, some of which had a national reach. When she was hired, she specifically asked that she not be mentioned in any publicity about the school. The next day, she spoke with her principal and reminded him of her request. He was confused, stating that he was only sharing good news. I had prompted her to explain her request, which she did. Several years earlier, she had been stalked and had moved out of state to escape the perpetrator. She was still concerned he would find her, and she did not want any information sent out. Her principal immediately removed all postings and assured her he would not repeat the action.

What If . . .

I made a mistake in terms of language with a social media post. It wasn't incorrect; it was unclear, but it could be interpreted in a negative way. I immediately deleted it and reposted it with clear, positive writing, but I inadvertently offended several people. What now?

Apologize. We've all sent an email or posted something before reviewing it and making changes. If you know who is offended, reach out to them individually to talk about the post. Your response, now that you know about the reaction to the post, is what counts. Listen attentively to what they have to say, be clear that you are sorry for the post and most of all, be sincere in your apology.

Building a Communicator Network

A network is a group of people who agree to work together with the focus on a common goal. Having a communication network allows you to maximize the effectiveness of your communication. Remember, communication is a two-way street, so this group will serve two purposes: to help you understand how stakeholders in various groups perceive a situation and to help you communicate your message.

One model is the Key Communicator Network, developed by the National School Public Relations Association. It includes a series of steps that help you identify key people to invite to participate and ideas for how you can work with them to advocate for your vision.

Building a Key Communicator Network

1. Convene a small group of trusted people who know the community. Brainstorm with those whom others listen to. While the bank president may be an opinion leader, so might the barber, cab driver, bartender or supermarket checkout clerk.
2. Create a workable list from all the names that have been gathered to invite to join your network. Make sure that all segments of the community are represented.
3. Send a letter to the potential members, explaining that you want to create a new communications group for your school to help the community understand the challenges, successes and activities of your school. In the letter, invite the potential members to an initial meeting and include a response form.
4. Make follow-up phone calls to those who do not return the response form, especially those who will be most important to have on your network.

5. Start the initial meeting by explaining that those in the audience have been invited because you see them as respected community members who care about the education students are being provided. Also, point out that you believe schools operate best when the community understands what is taking place and becomes involved in providing the best possible learning opportunities for students. Then, describe the objectives of a Key Communicator Network:

   To provide network members with honest, objective, consistent information about the school.
   - To have the network members deliver this information to others in the community when they are asked questions or in other opportunities.
   - To keep their ears open for any questions or concerns community members might have about the school. Those concerns should be reported to the principal or person in charge of the network so communication efforts can deal with those concerns. (It's always best to learn about concerns when one or two people have them instead of when 20 or 30 are vocally sharing them with others.)

   Ask the invitees for a commitment to serve on the network, and find out the best way to communicate with them (i.e., email, text, social media or even phone).
6. Establish a Key Communicator Network newsletter specifically for these people. After the first year, send out a short evaluation form to see how the network is working and might be improved.

For more information about Key Communicator Networks, contact the National School Public Relations Association at 301-519-0496 and purchase a copy of *A Guidebook for Opinion Leader/Key Communicator Programs*.

Now think about your own school community. How would you build a Key Communicator Network? Use the "Creating Your Key Communicator Network" chart to develop your plan.

Creating Your Key Communicator Network	
1. Who would you bring together to talk about building a network? Who would you talk with about the group? How would you assure all segments of your community are represented?	
2. How will you extend an invitation to potential members and explain the purpose of the group? How will you create a sense of urgency and importance for their participation?	
3. How do you plan to organize the initial meeting? Where will the meeting be held? How will you share your vision? How will you listen and gather feedback from members?	
4. How will you organize your work? Will you use a private Facebook group, a shared document system such as Dropbox or live sessions such as Microsoft Teams?	
5. What process will you use to both gather and share information with the network? How will you keep members engaged in the work?	

Who Are My Audiences?

There are several types of groups you will want to communicate with. On a local level, there are both internal and external stakeholders.

Internal	External
Teachers Staff Students Administrative team PTAs/PTOs Other leaders in the district School board	Families Community movers and shakers Nonprofits Media Business leaders Senior citizens Local college Community colleges

You'll communicate with all of these groups, perhaps at different times and for different purposes. Using your communication network can facilitate your partnership with each.

We'd like to specifically address a third group: local, state and national elected officials. In a remote learning environment, we've found that many decisions have been taken out of the hands of school officials and are being determined by elected officials. For example, during the COVID-19 pandemic, state governors either recommended or mandated school decisions. Due to this, it's important for us to understand how to communicate with elected officials.

Communicating With Elected Officials

- ♦ Comprehensive knowledge of issues and process.
- ♦ Know elected officials and staff.
- ♦ Effective communicator.
- ♦ Commitment to partnership.
- ♦ Constant communication.
- ♦ Balance competing priorities.
- ♦ Take time for little things.

Comprehensive Knowledge

Effective communicators have a comprehensive knowledge of the legislative and appropriation processes. Both processes are intricate and require that you understand the "ins and outs." If you don't understand the processes, it's nearly impossible to be successful. For example, you know when during the legislative year bills get introduced or you understand how committee hearings work.

Know Elected Officials

Communicators also need to know their elected officials, as well as their staff and their "gatekeepers." A meeting with the official is essential, but you want to be more than a casual acquaintance. You want the visit to help you develop a relationship. Often, these relationships mean that you are seen as trustworthy and someone who can be relied upon for good, solid information.

You must also know the legislator's staff and their "gatekeepers." When Barbara's dad went to Washington, DC, to visit elected officials on "lobby" days for a professional association, it was apparent that time with the official was at a premium. His first visit with a senator lasted for five minutes before the senator was called to the Senate floor for a vote. He did refer her dad to a staff member who handled education issues. The staff member gave him 30 minutes for a full discussion of his issue. This meeting opened the door for future meetings, emails and calls.

What If . . .

Is it really worth my time to communicate with my elected officials? Sometimes it seems they have their minds made up.

There's always a lot of posturing by elected officials. We've learned that the best way to influence officials is by being proactive, getting to know them before there is a critical issue you want to deal with, build a relationship with their staff and provide them with clear, concise background information and talking points. It's always a good idea to describe examples of how the issue affects voters in their community. Elected officials are always thinking about the next election and don't want to be on the wrong side of an issue important to their constituents.

Effective Communicator

To be an effective communicator, a communicator must have a grasp of the total issue, which includes all sides of the issue. The ability to understand the varying aspects of an issue while still lobbying for the desired outcome is important. Effective communication for a communicator also includes presenting the issue without exaggerating and using local needs and stories to support your points.

Commitment to Partnership

Lobbying requires working with those on both sides of the aisle or issue. You'll need to partner with like-minded individuals but also those who differ with you. You may not always agree, but there are times you can come to a consensus. Without support that goes beyond those who agree with you, you may not accomplish your goals. Partnering through collaboration is an essential component for effective lobbying.

Constant Communication

Communication is a two-way street, but effective communicators stay in constant communication with elected officials and their staff without being a nuisance. In the next section, we'll look at 15 ways to keep in touch with elected officials.

Balance Competing Priorities

Many priorities demand a communicator's attention. The key to being an effective communicator is the ability to balance those demands.

Take Time for Little Things

Along with balancing competing priorities, effective communicators take time to process what is happening and reflect on their progress, strengths and challenges. They use this to plan for the future. Finally, an effective communicator never forgets to say thank you, whether it is verbally or in writing.

What Are My Platforms for Communication?

We should also consider how we will communicate with teachers, families and other stakeholders. Let's look at traditional options and social media outlets.

Social Media

Social media has become one of the nation's most important tools for communication, and most school leaders recognize the power of social media to shape and mold public opinion. A recent study found that most principals believe that social networking can positively affect their communication. Almost every school has a presence on social media. In addition, school districts maintain their own social media presence.

While it is easy to dismiss social networking as a fascination of teenagers and college students, to do so minimizes one of the fastest-growing trends in technology: the ability to easily and quickly connect with others and with information about groups and organizations. For example, you may have seen Dr. Quentin Lee's parody video of MC Hammer's song "U Can't Touch This." The Alabama principal rewrote the lyrics into a coronavirus awareness song, which quickly went viral.

For many schools, their online presence has evolved beyond the school website and often includes several social media sites. A school Facebook page (www.facebook.com), Twitter account (www.twitter.com), Instagram account (http://instagram.com), YouTube channel (www.youtube.com) or Flickr account (www.flickr.com) are common. One of the advantages of these sites is that they are free. But one of the challenges is the need to maintain and update your presence on these sites.

Why a Social Media Presence?

Social media can help create a community where your students, teachers, families and community can gather and share information, interact and build your school's image and reputation. That's a powerful tool for communication.

Increasingly, families and community turn to online resources as a way to learn about schools and other educational organizations, to identify their strengths and challenges and to assist in making decisions about school programs and placement.

Having a presence on social media helps to establish your school as one that is comfortable with a more transparent presence and allows you to more quickly disseminate information about your school. Always build a link to your school's social media sites from your main website.

Facebook

Facebook has become the most frequently used social media site for youth and adults. A presence on Facebook helps to build your school's image as one that is comfortable with a more transparent communication presence. Because of its wide use, it is easy for families to connect and receive information about your school.

Twitter

Another powerful social media tool is Twitter. Each entry is limited to no more than 140 characters and is based on a simple concept: that people want to know what others are doing. It is a way to provide short updates and deliver those updates quickly and efficiently to followers of your Twitter account.

People use Twitter to communicate, ask directions, seek advice, share ideas and information and exchange thoughts. Schools and other businesses increasingly use Twitter to make announcements and share important news.

As with Facebook, Twitter has the option of a corporate Twitter account, one used commonly by schools. These accounts provide a way to enhance an online presence while having greater control over the message and the image. One of the major advantages of a corporate Twitter account is the ability to prevent unwanted tweets from being published, those that may detract from your school and your message.

With a Twitter account your school can quickly provide followers with up-to-date information about things like school closing, student activities, awards and recognitions and upcoming events for parents. It is a great way to share the accomplishments of your students and your teachers.

> **9 Ways Your School Can Use Twitter**
> - Tweet photos and brief biographies about new teachers.
> - Share information about new programs.
> - Post your school's sports scores and results.
> - Post changes to your schedule.
> - Announce upcoming meetings and events.
> - Share educational news and articles about your school and program.
> - Tweet a school photo of the day.
> - Post short videos about school concerts or drama performances.
> - Tweet recognitions and awards for students and staff.

A Twitter account is a great advocacy tool and a way to share information with families and the community. Increasingly, parents and other stakeholders use their mobile phones to access their Twitter account and stay in touch with friends. This provides almost simultaneous access to parents and others and provides one way to nurture and sustain your school's relationship with these groups. Don't forget to establish a link between your school's website and your Twitter account.

Instagram, YouTube, TikTok and Flickr

In addition to a presence on Facebook and Twitter, many schools use Instagram (http://instagram.com), YouTube (www.youtube.com), TikTok (www.tiktok.com) or Flickr (www.flickr.com) for posting photos or videos of school events. All sites are free and provide a quick and easy way to store and share information about your school.

You can also build links between both sites and other communication tools like your school's website or your Facebook and Twitter account.

Nine Ways Your School Can Use Instagram, YouTube, TikTok and Flickr

Ways to Use YouTube or TikTok for School Communications

- Post a video of school concerts and dress rehearsals.
- Share a video of a recent athletic event.
- Post a video orientation to your school.
- Create a video that introduces your new teachers.
- Share a safety video for use in science labs.

Ways to Use Flickr and Instagram for School Communications

- Share photos from recent school activities.
- Create a photo library about recognitions and awards your school receives.
- Post a school photo of the day or week.
- Create a photo orientation packet to introduce your school to new students and their families.

Dealing With Rumors on Social Media

One of the detriments of social media is the ability to spawn rumors. They are quickly spread via texts, Twitter, Facebook and other sites and can quickly overwhelm your ability to respond. Often they will take on a life of their own and, accurate or not, require a response. For many school leaders, the issue is when and how to address rumors and put them to rest. The National School Public Relations Association (2010) posed that question to principals and identified some interesting approaches:

- It is important to make a cognitive rather than emotional response to rumors. So, when responding, provide only the facts and make sure information is both timely and accurate.

- Assure families, students and the community that you are aware of the rumor, are investigating and will deal with it appropriately.
- Ask for specific details about rumors people have heard. This can help with your assessment and response.
- When things change quickly, and they often do with remote learning, communicate promptly. Have a system in place to notify parents and the community. Many schools ask parents to share their email or mobile phone number so they can email or text them with information.
- Create a "Fact Check" site on your school's website or social media site and let people know this is where they can go either to post a rumor or to get a response. Monitor this site often so that you stay ahead of the rumors.
- Recognize the importance of redundant dissemination of information. Everyone doesn't get their information from the same source (Williamson & Johnston, 2012).

Traditional Media

There are lots of ways to gather information. Social media has become the norm for many families, but traditional media, including television, radio, print media and the Internet, continues to provide information and be accessed by some families. Often these sources are used when families look for more detailed information or the background on a decision after they've consulted social media.

The traditional media has many forms that include local and state newspapers, television, radio and magazines. These sources are good for sharing information like your plan to reopen schools or an in-depth story about your remote learning curriculum. They are less useful for disseminating information quickly in response to a crisis or rapidly changing conditions.

Changing Media Environment

In the past, media operated with fixed datelines and a fixed publication schedule. While that is true for some media outlets, almost all newspapers, television and radio outlets have an online presence. Online sites are continuously updated with new stories and information. In fact, for most major publications, stories are published online before they appear in print.

Throughout southeastern Michigan, as well as other states, local newspapers are disappearing. Recently the entire chain of local papers in the Detroit area converted to an online format. Similarly, the *Ann Arbor News* switched from daily print publication to twice a week print editions while offering a comprehensive online edition available at no cost to local readers. Perhaps more important for advocacy, readers are able to comment on stories, and those comments, right or wrong, get wide dissemination among the public.

These changes are just another manifestation of the changing media environment at the local, state and national level. This means information will continue to be distributed faster and more broadly than at any time in the past.

A Final Note

Effective communication skills are critical for school leaders to effect change. Understanding the key characteristics of general and online communication, then applying those skills in traditional and social media outlets, will help you accomplish your goals.

Points to Ponder
How does this information apply to my current situation?
What are two to three key points to remember?
What is one action step I would like to take?

References

Blackburn, B. (2020). *Rigor in the remote learning classroom: Instructional tips and strategies*. Routledge.

Blackburn, R., Blackburn, B., & Williamson, R. (2018). *Advocacy from A to Z*. Routledge.

National School Public Relations Association. (2010). *Dealing with rumors spawned by text messages*. http://nspra.org/node/3072

National School Public Relations Association. (2020). *A guidebook for opinion leader/key communicator programs*. NSPRA.

Williamson, R., & Blackburn, B. (2016). *The principalship from A to Z* (2nd ed.). Routledge.

Williamson, R., & Blackburn, B. (2018). *Rigor in your school: A toolkit for leaders* (2nd ed.). Routledge.

Williamson, R., & Blackburn, B. (2019). *Seven strategies for improving your school*. Routledge.

Williamson, R., & Johnston, J. H. (2012). *The school leader's guide to social media*. Routledge.

6

Instructional Leadership in a Remote Learning Setting

The responsibility for quality instruction resides with the school principal. It is a key function of the principalship. That doesn't change with remote learning. The principal continues to play an important role in creating a climate where conversations about instruction are common and part of the everyday operation of the school. Of course, the tools may be a little different due to remote learning, but the emphasis remains the same. It's about supporting teacher work and promoting conversations about student learning and their teaching. There are several key behaviors of effective instructional leaders.

The Effective Instructional Leader
- Understands that teachers are adults and respond well to the principles of adult learning.
- Recognizes that teachers have varied comfort levels with technology and remote learning and should not be treated alike.

> - Supports the needs of teachers at different stages of their career cycle, recognizing that younger teachers may be more comfortable with remote learning and more experienced teachers less so.
> - Helps teachers to understand and learn from their teaching experiences.
> - Is empowering and motivating.
>
> *Adapted from:* Glickman et al. (2018)

Principals who are the most effective instructional leaders work collaboratively with teachers to support the integration of reflective practice and professional learning into school practices. They:

- Acknowledge the difficulties of growing and changing, including the natural resistance to change and the risk-taking that is involved
- Talk openly, and frequently, with teachers about instruction, make suggestions, give feedback, and solicit teachers' advice and opinions about classroom instruction
- Develop cooperative, nonthreatening partnerships with teachers and promote group development that is characterized by trust, openness and freedom to make mistakes
- Model effective teaching skills, including use of varied technology tools, when working with their staff and acknowledge that they are also learning about remote learning
- Support development of coaching skills and reflective conversations among educators

Finally, principals who are instructional leaders understand that there are significant differences between a novice teacher in the first year of his or her career and a veteran teacher who has been recognized for his or her skilled instruction. They also know that their interaction with that teacher can either promote or inhibit professional learning in their school.

In this chapter, we are going to look at four aspects of instructional leadership.

> Building relationships
> Providing support
> Coaching
> Hiring teachers

Building Relationships in a Remote Setting

Building a positive relationship with your teachers is key to your success as an instructional leader. Although this is always true, it is even more important during remote learning. Many of the informal ways we build relationships with teachers, such as dropping by a classroom during planning period or checking with a teacher when you see them in the hall, cannot take place in remote learning. Therefore, we must work harder to create or strengthen positive relationships with our faculty. There are several helpful guidelines:

- **Clarify "Rules of Engagement"**—Talk with individual teachers about the frequency, means and ideal timing of communication about their work. Be sensitive to the constraints of remote work and the need for employees to balance demands for childcare and multiple work and learning schedules with their own work. For example, the end of the school day may not be the optimal time for an online supervisory meeting.
- **Establish and Maintain a Schedule of Interaction**—During a "check-in" with each teacher, talk about a schedule that would fit their remote learning classroom. Be respectful of the time and context of their classroom. It's likely that the daily schedule will vary. Find a mutually agreed-upon time for you to "sit in" on their synchronous instruction.

- **Personalize Meetings**—Be sure that every meeting is tailored to meet the needs of each individual teacher. Good supervisory practices take into account the content, grade level and experience of the teacher.
- **Assure Privacy**—Be respectful of the teacher's need for privacy about supervision and evaluation. Always meet one-on-one and defer to the teacher regarding location and setting. Webcams can be incredibly intrusive, and whether it's one's personal office or one's home, there may be things you don't want others to observe.
- **Focus on Support**—Most teachers are new to remote learning. It can be a steep learning curve. Always ask how you can support them. Be an active listener, but be comfortable asking for clarification if there's something you don't understand. Follow their lead when they identify challenges and be willing to help them problem-solve and resolve the issue.
- **Model Optimism and Drain Fear**—Teachers and other employees pay attention to the leader's behavior. When you talk, be sure to remain optimistic, provide examples of success and, as we mentioned, always offer support. Moving to a new remote learning model can create fear and anxiety. Your job is to drain away that fear and be encouraging and supportive.

Providing Support for Teachers During Remote Learning

The transition to remote learning has taken a toll on many teachers and other staff. They miss the opportunity to interact daily, the ability to talk in the hallway or stop into someone's room after school. An online meeting doesn't substitute for the friendly banter of a staff meeting or social gathering.

It's important to recognize the challenges of remote work. Remote workers often experience social isolation, disconnected from one another and from their principal. They also lack access to information or resources and in many cases are dealing with distractions from home, like dealing with childcare or even a location to do their work. The challenges are real, but there are things you can do to support your employees while working remotely (Larson et al., 2020).

- **Set Boundaries**—Studies show that remote workers often spend more time working than when they are in a traditional setting. Monitor your teachers to assure they, too, are assuring work–life balance. Remote learning does not mean responding to parents, or students, at all hours.
- **Clarify Ways to Connect**—Be clear about how you will connect with your team. One school used video conferencing for check-ins and other meetings but agreed to use texting when something was urgent. Also be clear about expectations for sharing information among your teachers. Identify a time during the day when employees can reach you.
- **Provide Lots of Information**—Remote employees often feel isolated and that they lack information. That's because the informal interaction that we take for granted in a physical school is missing in a virtual school. Provide regular updates even if you have little to update. Communication is one way to maintain connections among remote employees. At Ron's university, the president sends every employee a weekly COVID update. Parts of it are repetitious, reminding everyone of important safety protocols, but each week the staff is updated on action the university is taking to support remote instruction, modify classrooms in preparation for the return of face-to-face instruction and share good news from across the campus.
- **Use Multiple Communication Tools**—Mass emails to the entire faculty can distribute information quickly but is insufficient. Become familiar with, and use, a variety of communication strategies. One study found that people will be more engaged, and interactive, when using video to talk about their work. Video provides for visual cues and reduces the sense of isolation. It's far more personal than email or other written communication.

- **Monitor Nonverbal Behavior**—In online meetings, tone and voice serve as proxies for some of the other nonverbal feedback we receive when face-to-face. The inflection or pitch of the voice or even the frequency of comments can indicate the employee is experiencing some anxiety.
- **Gauge Engagement**—People have different levels of engagement in individual or team meetings. Be looking for changes in behavior. Is an employee less engaged than normal?
- **Minimize Social Isolation**—Loneliness and isolation are common complaints in remote work. Those informal connections mentioned earlier are missing. Many people build their own network and connect with friends and colleagues. But that often doesn't substitute for the interaction at work. Some leaders organize something called the "virtual water cooler" where their employees can meet online in a video conference site to just talk and catch up on each other's lives. The meetings are always voluntary. The key is to provide a quick update, under a minute, and then to ask something like "What do you have planned for the weekend?" or "What's going on with your . . . ?". One principal had a virtual pizza party by having pizza delivered to every teacher at the beginning of a video conference. They chatted about nonwork topics while they enjoyed their pizza. While these events sound "forced," they actually help reduce feelings of isolation.
- **Offer Encouragement and Emotional Support**—The research on emotional intelligence and emotional contagion says that employees look for cues about how to react to changes like moving to remote learning. If you communicate stress, that will "trickle-down" to your employees (Goleman, 2005). It is important to acknowledge the stress and anxiety that can come from an abrupt transition to remote learning. Listen to your employees and empathize with their concerns. Always listen carefully and let the employees' concerns be the focus of the conversation rather than your own. Also provide affirmation and express confidence in your team.

Next, since remote learning is particularly stressful for many teachers, you'll want to create an environment that is focused on your teachers, rather than on the challenges of working in remote locations.

> **Steps to Create a "People-Oriented" Workplace**
> - See each person as an individual, as unique.
> - Consider exceptions to the rules when appropriate, especially given the multiple roles employees juggle—teacher, parent, caregiver.
> - Value listening and respecting varied points of view.
> - Allow flexibility for people to teach or organize their remote classrooms in different ways as you would in face-to-face instruction.
> - Provide opportunities for leadership to everyone.

What If . . .

I have one or two teachers who have totally withdrawn from all interactions with me and other faculty. I know they are overwhelmed by remote learning and other stressors, but nothing seems to draw them out. I've tried a variety of ideas, and I've been able to connect remotely with everyone else. What do I do with these two teachers?

It's likely they haven't totally withdrawn but instead have reduced their interaction. If they have, you have a right to expect them to "check in" with you. Talk with them to learn about their life outside of work, as well as their remote learning experience. Be supportive and thank them for their efforts. However, if they will not communicate with you or if their work has deteriorated, you have a far more serious problem that must be immediately addressed. Be persistent but be supportive and understanding.

Coaching

Teachers value, and respond to, coaching and other opportunities to reflect on their own teaching. This collaborative approach engages teachers but, at the same time, doesn't reward less skillful teaching. Teachers value the chance to work with their principal and/or other teachers to analyze their instruction and develop plans for strengthening their practice. Similarly, teachers crave feedback and an opportunity to reflect on their work. Rather than resisting supervision, they seek authentic risk-free opportunities to talk about their teaching and to grow professionally.

Become a Powerful Coach for Remote Learning

The principal, rather than being the expert and telling a teacher what to do, serves as the "lead coach" responsible for engaging teachers in a process that respects them as learners and works with them to reflect on their teaching and identify ways to strengthen their practice. When principals serve as coaches, it is critical that the two roles remain separate and that clear boundaries be established about how information from coaching will be used. The evidence shows that teachers are able to separate the roles.

The primary role of the coach is to ask questions that are open-ended and promote cognition. Listening, probing for deeper meaning and being nonjudgmental are critical skills. Good coaching is built on a foundation of trust. It occurs when the coach creates an open, respectful and inviting setting. Coaching cannot be forced. Good coaches share several traits. They:

- **Enroll Teachers**—Coaching cannot be seen as punishment or as a requirement. Good coaches create a setting that welcomes teachers and in which teachers choose to participate.
- **Identify Teacher Goals**—A top-down approach rarely works. Good coaches help teachers identify goals for their work and support teachers' efforts to improve.

- **Listen**—Perhaps no other skill is as important as the ability to listen intently to those being coached. Good coaches create a setting where teachers feel comfortable, can be candid without fear of retribution and are curious and inquisitive.
- **Ask Thoughtful Questions**—Good coaches ask thoughtful, open-ended questions that promote reflection. They are interested in promoting teacher cognition rather than providing answers. You might also use appropriate prompts.

Acknowledgment prompts include "Tell me more," "I understand" or "I'm following you."

Reflective prompts you might use are "So, you would like...," "I think you're saying..." or "You feel...because...".

- **Provide Feedback**—Good coaches don't provide feedback in the traditional sense. They don't tell teachers what to do. But they are comfortable using data from an observation, or comments made by the teacher, to provide feedback. All feedback is precise and nonjudgmental. Good coaches are always open to the teacher's point of view (Garmston & Wellman, 2013; Hirsh & Killion, 2007).

Finally, there are specific conditions that can assist your coaching efforts.

Conditions for Successful Coaching

The conditions that support effective coaching include:

- Presume positive intentions.
- Talk with the teacher to identify a focus for the coaching. Assume the teacher can analyze and reflect on their teaching and identify an area for growth.

> - Ask clarifying questions to understand the context (students, content, prior learning), the lesson and the teacher's thinking about the design and delivery of the lesson.
> - Remain nonjudgmental.
> - Listen attentively and authentically; use paraphrasing to indicate that you are listening and understand what was said.

What If . . .

Sometimes teachers seem to struggle with my differing and shifting roles of supervisor and coach. How can I assure them that my coaching work is not part of their evaluation?

You're right about the mixed messages around a principal's work. Every principal wears multiple hats and sometimes the roles get confused. Most coaching is informal and not part of a defined program. It's often a conversation about what's occurring in the classroom, what's working or not working, and helping teachers identify ways to address the challenges. The best way to build confidence in your coaching is to not use what you learn in formal evaluations. Otherwise, people will not be candid with you. Reassure everyone about your coaching role and only work with those who volunteer. Once you've established yourself as a coach, others will choose to work with you.

Supporting Teachers Hired While Working Remotely

One characteristic of the pandemic has been an increase in turnover. Some teachers choose retirement rather than remote learning. Others take a leave of absence because of the need to balance other personal needs like childcare and caregiving for loved ones.

Even in the best schools, turnover among staff is growing. Hiring is often guided by district policies. You'll work closely with the human resources department about procedures for hiring in a remote setting.

The only difference in hiring when working remotely is the tools that you will use to review and screen applicants and then interview the finalists. Fortunately, there are technology tools that can assist in this process.

While new hires are more likely to be comfortable with a variety of technology tools, few will have actual remote learning experience. In addition to the general characteristics, be sure to have a list of descriptors of an effective remote learning instructor.

Characteristics of an Effective Remote Learning Teacher

Uses technology platforms to address standards and increase student learning.

Is proficient in technology that allows him or her to meet students' needs.

Incorporates student engagement in both synchronous and asynchronous learning opportunities.

Uses technology tools to help students organize their own learning and shift to independence.

Nurtures an online community and is an active participant in that community.

Onboarding New Teachers

Hiring a new teacher is only the start. You'll need to consider how to onboard your teachers, which is the process of supporting new employees when they join a company. For principals, it is how to welcome and support new teachers when their school is operating in remote learning.

Virtual onboarding has a special set of challenges. There may be no physical classroom for the teacher, or they may not have been there yet. They don't have the opportunity to meet formally, or informally, with grade or content colleagues. They may be unfamiliar with the formal, and informal, norms and operations of the school.

So, what do you do? We've identified some of the best advice from principals and other leaders who welcomed new teachers while working remotely.

- **Establish Personal Connections**—Often a new employee is shown around the school and introduced to other teachers, or they might be introduced in a staff meeting. Leverage virtual meeting tools to introduce new teachers. In Chapter 3 we shared an example of a principal who invited every new teacher, as well as the veterans, to create a short video introduction.
- **Assign a Mentor or Coach**—Identify another staff member or a grade/content team to assist the new teacher in learning the curriculum and/or locating instructional resources.
- **Assure IT Support**—Most new teachers have no experience with remote teaching. It's just not part of most university preparation programs. Make sure the teacher knows how to contact IT for needed support. You might ask your school's IT contact to proactively reach out and ask the teacher how they can be of assistance.
- **Virtual Celebrations and Recognitions**—Be attentive to scheduling of events like recognition of birthdays or other celebrations so that the new teacher is included in those events.
- **Encourage Wellness**—Many teachers and other staff struggled with the transition to remote learning. The rapid transition and the uncertainty of it all raised anxiety and disrupted established routines in both their personal and professional lives. In response, some districts created virtual mindfulness and wellness resources for their staff. Assure that your new teachers know about these resources and encourage their use when appropriate.

- **How to Get Help**—Make sure new teachers know how to get help if needed. Let them know how to contact you, or others in your office, if they have questions or need assistance.

Final Thoughts

Embracing your role as an instructional leader is important to build success in remote learning. Building and strengthening relationships, supporting and coaching teachers in a variety of ways and both hiring and ensuring the success of new teachers are all aspects of instructional leadership.

Points to Ponder

How does this information apply to my current situation?
What are two to three key points to remember?
What is one action step I would like to take?

References

Garmston, R., & Wellman, B. (2013). *The adaptive school: A sourcebook for developing collaborative groups* (2nd ed.). Christopher-Gordon.

Glickman, C., Gordon, S., & Ross-Gordon, J. (2018). *Supervision and instructional leadership: A developmental approach* (10th ed.). Pearson.

Goleman, D. (2005). *Emotional intelligence: Why it can matter more than iQ.* New York: Bantam Books.

Hirsh, S., & Killion, J. (2007). *The learning educator: A new era for professional learning.* Learning Forward.

Larson, B., Vroman, S., & Makarius, E. (2020). A guide to managing your (newly) remote workers. *Harvard Business Review.*

https://hbr.org/2020/03/a-guide-to-managing-your-newly-remote-workers

Williamson, R., & Blackburn, B. (2016). *The principalship from A to Z* (2nd ed.). Routledge.

Williamson, R., & Blackburn, B. (2018). *Rigor in your school: A toolkit for leaders* (2nd ed.). Routledge.

Williamson, R., & Blackburn, B. (2019). *Seven strategies for improving your school*. Routledge.

7

Providing Essential Professional Development Remotely

In today's changing world, providing professional development in a virtual setting is becoming more commonplace. In many cases, it is our only viable option, and in others, it is simply preferred due to convenience. Let's look at a model for planning professional development, ways to assess professional development and sample strategies you can use with your teachers.

Planning

In order to offer the most effective options for teachers, we must consider three aspects of professional development: the purpose, the content and the delivery platform.

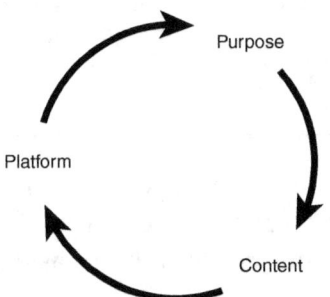

Determine Your Purpose

As you plan professional development, you will want to be sure that it links to your specific goals. Too often, we've seen schools jump on the latest bandwagon, which doesn't link to their school's focus. The best way to plan staff development is to assess your goals and needs first, then find professional development that supports them.

Sample Goal(s) and Need(s)	*Sample Professional Development*
Improve the quality of our remote instruction.	Interactive synchronous professional development presentations on how to use our platform most effectively to affect student learning
Ensure equity for all students	How to provide resources, including alternative options, for students in need How to provide opportunities for learning for those with limited Internet access How to reach disenfranchised parents and families

It's also critical that you assess your student data as part of the planning process to ensure your needs are met. Consider using a wide range of data, both numerical data and narrative data.

Numerical Data	*Narrative Data*
Student grades or test scores Student engagement time on electronic platform Student, parent and staff survey compilation School climate assessment Instructional practices data from observations Curriculum audit results Report of alignment with state or national standards	Anonymous comments from peer observations or learning walks Teachers' self-assessment summaries of student feedback Comments related to numerical data (climate assessment, curriculum audit, standards alignment) Results of electronic focus groups with parents and families

Finally, any professional development should be research based. I spoke with a principal recently who was excited about a new initiative for the school. When I asked her what research it was based on, she said, "I know several other schools that are using it, so it must be good." Effective professional development is based on solid research. How do I know if something is research based? Professional development should be research based; use research that is objective, not subjective; utilize observations and measurements that are reliable and valid; and be able to be replicated and generalized.

Samples of Research-Based Professional Development

Cognitive task analysis.
Response to intervention.
Jigsaw method.
Classroom discussion.
Scaffolding.

From: https://visible-learning.org/hattie-ranking-influences-effect-sizes-learning-achievement/

What If . . .

Our school was focused on three major goals prior to remote learning. Now, we probably have another three. All six are important. How do we prioritize?

Remote learning changed a lot of things, including the focus of professional development. Ask your school improvement team or other collaborative group to help with prioritizing. We suspect that things directly related to technology, including the remote learning platform, will quickly emerge as more important. That's because they're urgent. Remember that you need to attend to those "basic needs" first. Then your staff will be ready to return to the things you were focused on prior to the pandemic.

Determine Your Content

The content you provide will be based on your goals as well as teachers' needs. However, we'd like to consider another aspect of determining your content: teachers' needs based on Maslow's hierarchy. Until we meet teachers' basic needs, it is difficult to move to the higher levels.

First, teachers have survival needs. In that level, teachers are concerned with issues such as *Do I have the right tools? Am I able to use the technology correctly?* Once those needs are satisfied, you'll want to turn your attention to security needs. These include *Where will I set up my computer for video presentations? How will I balance my work and personal life? Who is deciding how long we will do this?* Third, teachers have belonging needs. In this stage, they ask questions such as *How will I work with other teachers?* Closely linked to belonging are those related to esteem, such as *Will parents think I am a good teacher? Will students think I am a good teacher?*

Once all those needs are satisfied, you can move to working with the need for knowledge. Teachers are interested in topics such as *What should remote instruction look like? How do I plan a remote lesson? How do I incorporate scaffolding into remote lessons? What grading and assessment strategies are used?* This is the area you should focus on in your professional development, but it is important to address safety, security, belonging and esteem needs so that teachers will be able to concentrate on the content of your professional development.

Need as Identified by Maslow	Example of Staff Needs	Example of Remote Learning Needs
Aesthetic need (self-actualization)	Attention to the needs of students first	I am confident that I know what to do and how to do it. My students are my first priority.
Need for understanding	Focus on the developmental needs of students	Focus on all the knowledge issues here, but with an emphasis on understanding how to implement each effectively to meet the needs of all students.
Need for knowledge	Professional development: Program models Planning skills Curriculum	What should effective remote instruction look like? How can I plan a remote lesson that works for my students?

Need as Identified by Maslow	Example of Staff Needs	Example of Remote Learning Needs
	Instructional strategies Diversity issues Assessment strategies	*How do I scaffold in remote lessons for my struggling students?* *How do I ensure equity for all students?* *How do I grade fairly?*
Esteem needs	Will I be successful? Will I be valued?	*Will I do a good job?* *Will parents think I am a good teacher?* *Will students think I am a good teacher?* *Will I be able to use technology effectively?* *Will my administrators and other teachers think I am doing a good job?*
Belonging needs	Will I fit in? How can I connect with others?	*How will I work with other teachers?* *When will there be time and how will I connect with others?* *How will I know I am part of the group since we aren't physically together?*
Security needs	Where will I be working? Where will my room or office be located? What will my work look like? Who's making these decisions?	*Where will I set up my computer for video presentations?* *How will I balance my work and personal life?* *Who is deciding how long we will do this?*
Survival needs	Will I continue to have a job? Will I have the skills for the job? Will I have sufficient and appropriate materials?	*Will I continue to have a job?* *Do I have the right tools?* *Am I able to use the technology correctly?*

Determine the Platform

The best staff development is active, rather than passive. No one wants to listen to a lecture, being told what he or she is doing wrong and what he or she should change. Teachers want professional development that is positive and relevant to their needs, and they want to engage in learning in active ways. It's interesting to me that we promote active learning for students, but oftentimes we do the opposite for teachers. This is one of the reasons teacher input during planning is important. Teachers are very quick to ask questions to ensure active learning and relevance.

There are three questions to consider when choosing your platform for professional development.

> ***Three Questions***
> 1. What platform(s) will match our goals and needs?
> 2. How does the platform provide interaction and collaboration?
> 3. How does the platform provide follow-up opportunities?

There are several ways to address these questions. For example, if a grade level, team or department would like to look at student work to determine a common level of rigor or grading standards, you'll want a platform that encourages full collaboration. One school district used Google Docs to post work samples for review; then teachers met using Google Hangouts to discuss what they learned and any adjustments that needed to be made. Revised work was posted again for teachers to see.

Many districts prefer to use a book study, which allows teachers to share their learning on a common topic. This is one of the easiest professional development opportunities to shift online. Teachers and leaders can read ebooks and respond to the book via secure chat boards or blogs or discuss their reading via Zoom. If they incorporate strategies in their virtual classroom, they can post short videos or screenshots on a program like Canvas.

Finally, you may choose to use a content expert to present information to your teachers. A live presentation using Zoom, Google Hangouts, Skype Meet Now or Microsoft Teams is ideal, because the presenter can answer questions. You would also want to encourage the use of interactive tools such as breakout rooms, polls and chats so teachers are able to interact throughout the presentation.

Professional Learning Communities

Almost every school has a structure in place for involving teachers and other staff in school improvement activities. Often they're called a professional learning community (PLC), and the term is common in many schools. A PLC is one way to think about working collaboratively on your virtual learning program. PLCs take many forms and have different tasks, but are almost uniformly focused on improving student learning.

Central to the vitality of a professional learning community is a value on collaborative activity supported by professional development. The central focus is on continuous improvement with a results orientation. One principal described it as a "laser light focus on getting the desired results."

Focus of Successful Professional Learning Communities

- Continuous program improvement.
- Rigorous, relevant curriculum and instruction.
- Interdisciplinary teaching and instructional teams.

Adapted from: Oxley et al. (2006)

The remainder of this chapter will discuss seven professional development strategies that reflect strong PLCs. Each is collaborative, and each is focused on improved student learning.

Options for Professional Development in a Remote Setting

There are a variety of options for remote professional development other than synchronous workshops. Let's look at seven.

> **Remote Professional Development**
> Book study.
> Lesson studies.
> Discussing high expectations.
> Feedback loops.
> Learning walks.
> Unconferences.
> Personal action plans.

Book Study

A good way to engage people in their own professional learning is to organize a book study group. At some schools, every teacher is asked to read the same book and work in small groups to discuss the book and its implications for practice. At other schools, teachers may choose from several books and join colleagues who selected the same book for their discussion.

Some schools use technology for book study groups. For example, at Brookings-Harbor High School in Oregon, book study was a part of their annual professional development plan. Rather than meet in small groups on campus where one or two people might dominate the discussion, they used Moodle (http://mooodle.org), open-source software that is free and readily available online. With Moodle it is possible to create small discussion groups using threaded discussions. Each member of the groups can make comments and respond to the comments of others. Teachers reported that not only did participation increase but the quality of the discussion improved. One of the benefits is that teachers were able to participate any time of the day, at their convenience. That provided for more engaging and thoughtful discussion.

> **Book Study Protocol**
> ♦ Membership should be voluntary, but inclusive.
> ♦ Decide on a meeting schedule, meeting place, length of book to be read and what will happen after the book

is read. It is recommended that meetings last no more than one hour and be held at a consistent time and place.
- ◆ Select a responsible facilitator to keep the group on task and help manage the meetings.
- ◆ Select a book with a clear objective in mind. For example, use *Motivating Struggling Learners: 10 Strategies for Student Success* to address issues related to students who lack motivation about learning.
- ◆ Conversation is important in a book study. Members of the group share insights, ask questions about the text and learn from others. It is important to talk about how the ideas can be applied directly in the classroom and how to overcome any potential obstacles.
- ◆ Journaling is a useful way for members to think about their reading and reflect on how it might be used.

Lesson Studies

Lesson studies emphasize working in small groups to plan, teach, observe and critique a lesson. It's a tool that allows teachers to work together to improve instruction. It's an excellent reflection of the principles of professional learning communities, as the goal is to systematically examine your teaching in order to become more effective.

In a lesson study, teachers work together to develop a detailed plan for a lesson. One member of the group teaches the lesson to his or her students, while other members of the group observe. Next, the group discusses their observations about the lesson and student learning.

Teachers revise the lesson based on their observations, then a second group member teaches the lesson, with other members once again observing. Then, the group meets to discuss the revised lesson. Finally, teachers talk about what the study lesson taught them and how they can apply the learning in their own classroom.

In a remote setting you can't do physical observations of the lesson, but you can work collaboratively to develop and plan the lesson. After working together to develop the detailed plan, a member teaches the group virtually. If it is a synchronous lesson, perhaps teachers can attend to observe. If it is a recorded video, teachers can observe at their convenience. If it is a lesson in which students work independently to complete a task, other teachers review how the lesson is presented, as well as students' responses. From there, you follow the process, just virtually, with the adaptations. One caution—be sure you are addressing any student privacy issues.

Lesson studies allow teachers to collaboratively refine implementation of strategies so that you can all improve your remote teaching.

What If . . .

Although my teachers see the benefits of a lesson study, some are nervous. Even though they will plan together, one teacher is "observed" and critiqued. How can I help?

> Even confident and skilled teachers are sometimes reluctant to be so transparent about their teaching. Honor that reticence and begin with volunteers. We've worked with many schools who use lesson study, and that's almost always how they begin. Work with the staff to assure a safe way for sharing information with one another. Finally, be very clear that nothing in lesson study is evaluative. You may want to assure them that none of the information is shared with you. It's only for the team.

Discussing Expectations

We've found that there are times when teachers have different expectations for how to implement specific state and national standards. When teachers are using the same standards but may have different expectations for student learning related to the standards, it's important to develop a plan for greater consistency.

Protocol for a Conversation About Expectations

Step 1: Post copies of a standard assignment, such as a short essay, completed by students. Be sure to have copies from several teachers.

Step 2: Ask everyone to assess it.

Step 3: Meet synchronously using a program such as Google Hangouts. Use prompts to guide the discussion. For example, "How do you determine quality?" "What do you consider in a quality assignment?" or "What do you expect students to know in order to complete this assignment?"

Step 4: You may want to extend the conversation to other grade levels. Discussion prompts might include "What are some areas that students struggle with?" or "What do you expect students to know before they come into your class?"

Feedback Loops

One strategy Barbara uses with teachers is a feedback loop, which works for a variety of purposes, such as ensuring rigorous work, discussing incorporation of technology or ensuring appropriate levels of student engagement.

In a feedback loop, teachers start with an individual reflection on a work sample, whether it is on a lesson plan, assignment, sample of student work or video. Using a reflective guide, each teacher reviews the product in a shared document system such as Dropbox.

Reflective Guide	
Students' Instructional Needs	
What are the aspects of the product (lesson plan, assignment, work sample, video) that you believe meet the instructional needs of your students?	
What are the aspects of the product (lesson plan, assignment, work sample, video) that you believe need to be adjusted to meet the instructional needs of your students?	
Students' Developmental Needs	
What are the aspects of the products that meet the developmental needs of your students?	
What are the aspects of the products that need to be adjusted to meet the developmental needs of your students?	
Match With Standards	
What are the aspects of the product that you believe match the standards, assessments and preparation for the next grade level, college or career?	
What are the aspects of the product that you believe need to be adjusted to match the standards, assessments and preparation for the next grade level, college or career?	
Other Notes	
Questions	

Following the individual reflection, teachers meet synchronously in a discussion platform in pairs or small groups, whether by grade level, interdisciplinary team or subject area departments. Teachers share the product, as well as their reflections, and ask for input from the group.

Group Summary Sheet		
Instructional Needs	Developmental Needs	Standards/Challenge
Other Thoughts or Questions		

Finally, the individual teacher or the group of teachers broadens their audience for electronic feedback and discussion. You may include teachers from the grade level below the grade level with the product, as well as the grade level above the product, using the same group summary guide. We find that broadening the grade level informs teachers' practice in a new and different way.

For example, Barbara worked with one group of fifth-grade teachers who were trying to determine if they needed to adjust their math instruction. The grade level agreed that the instruction was appropriate, although challenging, for their students. However, when meeting with the fourth-grade teachers, they discovered that the standards in question were introduced in fourth grade, so students should have entered fifth grade with some level of understanding. Then, sixth-grade teachers noted that although students began sixth grade with a basic understanding of the particular math concepts, there were some missing applications students should have been taught. The feedback from the other grade levels was critical to the fifth-grade teachers' understanding of needed adjustments.

Learning Walks

A learning walk is a form of instructional walkthrough, but is typically organized and led by teachers. Learning walks are not evaluative. They are not designed for individual feedback, but instead help participants learn about instruction and identify areas of strength as well as need.

Learning walks provide a "snapshot" of the instructional program at your school and allow teachers to discuss current and new ideas. A school in Chicago organized "I Spy" days. Teachers dropped in on classrooms for five to ten minutes in order to identify positive examples of instruction. Teachers came back together after school with their "detective notebooks" to share what they had seen. It was an invigorating experience for teachers, who said this was the first time they had a chance to look at other classrooms. As one teacher explained, "I don't get time to visit other teachers' classes. I learned so much, and I have two new ideas I want to implement tomorrow."

Obviously, when working remotely you can't do learning walks the same way. But one school in Connecticut adapted this to an electronic format. Teachers chose a particular area in their delivery platform, and with appropriate permissions, opened that area for other teachers to view. During a particular time, teachers electronically "visited" other classrooms, looked for key items and shared feedback in a synchronous session using Microsoft Teams. Always respect the privacy of students during these virtual classroom visits.

Learning Walks

1. Work with your staff to identify the purpose for your learning walk.
2. Develop and use a consistent tool for participants to use to record their observations and collect data.
3. Work collaboratively to develop a schedule.
4. Make sure everyone is clear on the guidelines for observations.
5. View the electronic "classroom" and ask the teacher any questions, using an appropriate electronic messaging format.
6. Immediately after the walk, ask participants to meet electronically to discuss what they learned.
7. Develop a plan for sharing the information and for using it to guide your continued school improvement work.

Unconferences

Unconferences, whether offered on-site or online, have become popular in recent years. Unconferences allow educators to collaborate around shared interests and build on each person's strengths. Rather than attending a structured conference with a detailed schedule and perhaps assigned or ticketed sessions, an unconference provides an opportunity for all participants to suggest or lead topical sessions. During the unconference, teachers drop in and out of sessions of interest, based on their personal needs. Some teachers prefer unconferences because it empowers them to lead other educators. Unconferences can occur for a school district, state, educational association or around a broad topic.

A set of suggestions for planning an unconference can be found at www.ncbi.nlm.nih.gov/pmc/articles/PMC4310607/.

Personal Action Plans

Another option is the use of personal action plans. These allow teachers to develop an individual or small-group plan to address their needs. Some districts use micro-credentialing, where teachers earn badges for completing certain learning modules or tasks. Many regional educational service centers also offer mini-courses with certification credit, which allow teachers to customize a plan. Additionally, teachers can build their own online personal learning networks, where teachers can develop a larger educational network based on their needs. For example, Twitter offers a variety of chats and groups on topics ranging from virtual learning to parent involvement to students with special needs, or Google Educator Groups (GEG) connects you with other Google educators in your state.

Possible Sources for Online Professional Learning Communities (as of September 2020)

Teachersconnect.com (free membership).
Share my lesson communities.
Other educational organizations that have interest groups.
Cybraryman.com provides links to a wide variety of groups, including Twitter groups.

A Final Note

The growth of virtual learning for students means we must also address virtual professional development for teachers. By considering our purpose, the content and the appropriate platforms to deliver content, we can provide the most effective professional development for our teachers.

Points to Ponder

How does this information apply to my current situation?
What are two to three key points to remember?
What is one action step I would like to take?

References

Blackburn, B. (2016). *Motivating struggling learners: 10 strategies for student success*. Routledge.

Hattie, J. (2018). 252 influences and effect sizes related to student achievement. *Visible Learning*. https://visible-learning.org/hattie-ranking-influences-effect-sizes-learning-achievement/

Oxley, D., Barton, R., & Klump, J. (2006). Creating small learning communities. *Principal's Research Review*, 1(6), 3.

Williamson, R., & Blackburn, B. (2016). *The principalship from A to Z* (2nd ed.). Routledge.

Williamson, R., & Blackburn, B. (2018). *Rigor in your school: A toolkit for leaders* (2nd ed.). Routledge.

Williamson, R., & Blackburn, B. (2019). *Seven strategies for improving your school*. Routledge.

8

Ensuring Equity During Remote Instruction

Across the country, most schools moved quickly to a remote learning model in response to the pandemic. The closure of school buildings reminded us of the role schools play in the lives of children. Schools are places where children learn, but they are also places of safety and stability, a source of regular meals and a place for building deep personal relationships with teachers and other staff.

Recently a television station in Detroit did a series on preparing for the new school year. One day the story focused on tips for parents to help their child succeed in the new school year. It suggested purchasing a new computer with the right webcam and microphone, use of external headsets, a new desk located in a private place in the home and speedy access to the Internet. That's all good advice. But the recommendations reflected a suburban, middle-class point of view and didn't reflect the reality for many families.

That's the challenge. Many of our most vulnerable students—those from low-income households, those who are homeless or with limited English skills or those with disabilities—face growing inequity in the educational system. In a comprehensive survey of teachers, 51% of teachers in high-poverty schools reported that "most students participated daily in online learning," while 84% agreed with that statement in more affluent schools (Barnum & Bryan, 2020). That's a dramatic difference.

Equity Challenges

We don't have a lot of research on best practices for addressing inequities or for even assuring a continuous and quality learning program during a pandemic. But through the help of Education Trust (2020), we can identify some critical issues that you should consider to address inequity in your own school community.

Access to Technology Devices—In many communities students do not have access to laptops or other electronic devices to participate in remote learning. Some families have access but not enough devices for every child to be online at the same time. Many schools have purchased and distributed devices to students and their families. There's an increasing recognition that to provide synchronous instruction there must be one device for every student, not one device for each family.

Access to Reliable, High-Speed Internet—Even when they have a device, many families lack access to reliable, high-speed Internet. While this problem affects low-income families, it also affects others. In one southeastern county that is home to a major research university, over 70% of families (8,000 households) in one rural school district lacked access to broadband Internet. The Lincoln Community Schools in Michigan applied for a grant from the United Way to purchase hotspots that could be provided to families lacking robust Internet access.

Structuring Instructional Time for Varying Access—Some schools provide remote learning using an asynchronous model, allowing students to complete their work without face-to-face time with teachers or other students.

Others adopted a synchronous model that allows time for teachers and students to be together in real time. While synchronous learning resembles traditional classrooms, some students may not have reliable Internet connections or may not be available at specific times due to family work schedules or multiple children and a single computer.

What If . . .

The notion of structuring time is a real struggle for my teachers. They feel like synchronous learning is important, but it just doesn't work for some students. I've recommended they record sessions, but they say that is not the same.

I suspect there are teachers on your staff who successfully use synchronous and asynchronous learning, including short videos. You might want to highlight their work or ask them to talk about how they manage the balance. We talked with an elementary principal in Washington State who shared this problem. He discovered that some of his teachers were reluctant to record lessons because they lacked confidence in the technology and thought they would appear awkward in the videos. Some also were concerned about privacy issues. So, he asked teachers to use a background of some sort when recording to address privacy and encouraged them to record a couple of short lessons and watch them but not post. That way they gained confidence. Once those issues were addressed, they were more willing to record lessons.

Support for Students With Disabilities and English Language Learners—The rights of students with disabilities to a free and appropriate education don't disappear when schools close and move to remote learning. Similarly, the needs of English language learners continue during closures. Schools must implement plans for continuity of services, and this may require specialized software or hardware and access to other services such as speech and language therapy, physical therapy and occupational therapy.

Providing Social and Emotional Support—Schools serve an important role in supporting the social and emotional development of students. Remote learning makes it more difficult to maintain relationships and support emotional well-being. Teachers play a critical role, but they will also need support for themselves as they deal with the challenges of their students and with the move to remote learning. We'll address this more at the end of the chapter.

What Do I Do?

As with most challenges, there is no single solution. But across the country school districts have identified strategies that address each of these concerns. Here are some strategies we've identified.

Recognize the Problem—It starts with recognizing that there is a problem. Middle-class teachers and principals even with the best of intentions often don't recognize the depth of the equity issue schools face. Talk with leaders of local social services or faith-based leaders about the families they serve. Ask for their help to identify the equity issues in your school. Also, use a chart similar to the one here to have teachers assess their students. Then search for solutions.

Assess Your Challentxges With Students				
Student Name _____ Date of Assessment _____				
Issue	High Need	Medium Need	Low Need	Notes
Access to technology				
Access to Internet/high-speed service				

Issue	High Need	Medium Need	Low Need	Notes
Other needed resources				
Ability to attend asynchronous learning sessions				
Access to school or district resources, such as speech therapy or mental health				
Access to needed support, such as that for students with special needs				
Need for social-emotional learning support				

Respond Affirmatively—Learn from your teachers about how frequently students participate in remote learning. Survey families about things like Internet access or access to computers. Many districts acquired tablets and provided them, loaded with software, to students and their families. Other districts acquired and distributed hotspots to provide families with Internet access.

Be Flexible With the Instructional Model—Balance instruction with flexibility between synchronous and asynchronous learning so that families have flexibility in scheduling learning. Acknowledge families have varied work schedules and that, particularly among younger students, childcare providers may be unable to provide for synchronous learning.

Provide Resources for Families—Provide families with resources to support their children's learning. That can be particularly helpful for families of students with disabilities. The Jefferson County Schools (Kentucky) provided families with video links to therapeutic activities for students, while the San Francisco Unified Schools (California) designed a website for families that included home learning activities created by speech, occupational and physical therapists.

Connect With Students and Families—Encourage teachers to provide time for students to personally connect with the teacher and with one another. The Phoenix Union High School District (Arizona) launched an "Every Student, Every Day" program where school staff reached out to all students on a daily basis to check in, answer questions and relay information. The Northshore Schools (Washington) built connection time into every Friday's schedule. Teachers focused on social-emotional learning and provided time for students to chat with one another. They continued some of their school's practices like Pajama Day or Favorite Team T-Shirt Day. In Chapter 9, you'll find a variety of other strategies for connecting with families.

Real-Life Examples

Although we have discussed many equity issues, we'd like to take several key ones and provide more detail on the problem and possible solutions.

> Internet access.
> Meals for eligible students.
> Childcare.

Internet Access

The Problem—It's hard to participate in a robust remote learning program when you lack Internet access. But that's exactly what many students face. In rural Virginia one district found that 40% of its students couldn't even get reliable Internet access at home. One district in southeastern Michigan found that nearly 70% of its rural students lacked access.

Strategies—There is no single strategy that resolves this issue. But some schools have used a variety of approaches to address it. For example, districts acquired mobile hotspots and distributed them to families. Local school foundations or other philanthropic groups provided the funds. Other districts turned school buses into hotspots and located them throughout the district. Still others worked with local libraries or museums to expand the reach of their Wi-Fi so it could be accessed from the parking lot. Yet other schools helped families with a subscription to a basic service plan from a local provider. One example is the Xfinity basic plan.

There are organizations that connect people to low-cost Internet and PCs. Two we found online are EveryoneOn (https://everyoneon.org), a nonprofit helping families with Internet access. Their website provides a tool kit schools can use to get information to families. The other is PCs for People (www.pcsforpeople.org) that helps connect families with affordable refurbished computers and low-cost mobile Internet.

The Saline Area Schools (Michigan) worked with local businesses and the Saline Area Schools Foundation to provide options for families. They worked with a company, Rural Reach (https://ruralreach.com), that helps rural families connect to the Internet. Their website (https://salinelive.org) provides information on their program and how families can apply for assistance. Basically, Saline Live staff work with families to find a workable solution.

Free and Reduced-Price Meals

The Problem—Approximately 26 million children in the United States qualify for free or reduced school meals. That's about half of all school-aged children. Districts are obligated to continue to provide this option for families. When remote learning first began, the U.S. Department of Agriculture granted waivers for the content of the meals and their distribution. Those may or may not continue during the new school year.

What If . . .

I don't have any control over meals in my district, but I have students with food scarcity. Do you have any ideas of other ways I can support them?

Food insufficiency is a real problem. First, your district must provide meals in some form, or they jeopardize their federal

> funds. Fortunately, there are other options. Contact your food bank and/or the United Way in your area. They can provide you with a list of resources. In some communities, local churches or mosques help with distribution of food. Finally, many local farmers markets or roadside markets prefer to donate food rather than throw it away.

Strategies—School districts developed a variety of ways to continue providing free and reduced-price meals to students. In some districts, bus drivers delivered meals. In others, meals were available for pick-up at the local elementary school or other designated location. But pick-up shifted the burden to families, and those families often lacked transportation. Schools in Jefferson County, Alabama, used a third-party delivery service to distribute meals directly to families. Meal distribution provides an opportunity to distribute information about the remote learning program and provide families with information related to other issues like Internet access or access to health care resources.

Childcare

The Problem—Many families struggle with childcare when their children are learning remotely. In some cases, parents are home because they're working at home. That means they're also busy and unable to monitor their children's schoolwork. In other families the parents must return to work. Families turn to grandparents or other extended family or friends. In some cases older children are left alone.

Strategies—As with the other equity issues, there is no single solution. But some novel alternatives have emerged. In some communities, friends or neighbors have organized study groups where children of a similar age are supervised by a single parent. They basically create their own circle of friends, their own pandemic bubble, where they interact only with a limited number of people.

The community education program in one Michigan district organized extended childcare. For many years they provided before-school and after-school programs for children and youth. This year they extended the concept to the school day.

The district mascot is the hornet, and so the program is called Hornet Homeroom. It supplements remote learning by providing a safe, socially distanced, mask-required setting for students in grades K–5. Students do their online instruction during the day. Supervisors monitor the students and assist with the use of technology but do not provide instruction. Basically, it's a staffed and supervised place for students to do their online instruction while parents are at work.

In Bozeman, Montana, where they are using a hybrid remote learning model, the United Way is doing something similar. They will staff six classrooms every day from 7:30 a.m. until 4:30 p.m. Parents can reserve a spot for their child on days when they don't have face-to-face instruction. The sites will be staffed and provide technical assistance but will not provide instruction.

In Portage, Michigan, the district is allowing students in middle school or high school to use the common areas of the school building, places like the cafeteria, library or lobby, to do their remote learning. Internet access is available and supervision is provided. Masks and social distancing are required. Teachers are off-site providing remote learning.

Students With Disabilities

The Problem—When schools quickly transitioned to remote learning, the education of students with disabilities was often disrupted. Schools struggled to continue services that were often very specific and required specialized hardware or assistive technology. Related services like speech and language therapy, occupational therapy, physical therapy and school psychology services became a challenge to provide.

Strategies—Like the other equity issues, there is no one solution and your district may have designed its own approach. Many districts used video conferencing to hold individual education plan (IEP) and 504 meetings remotely. Jefferson County Schools (Kentucky) provided families with online resources for therapeutic activities. The San Francisco Unified School District (California) created a website for families of students with disabilities. The site included activities for home learning that were created by speech, occupational and physical therapists and included activities that caregivers could use at home with students.

In Rock Hill, South Carolina, mental health and speech therapy specialists used teletherapy to provide services. The district's mental health providers conducted one-to-one and group sessions using Zoom.

Equipping Teachers to Teach in an Equitable Manner

One issue that is often overlooked is the need for teachers to fully understand issues and know how to address those concerns. We discussed professional development in Chapter 6, but providing ongoing resources for teachers is one way to address equity. There are a wide range of online sources you can use with teachers.

Teacher Resources for Addressing Equity in Online Learning

Culturally Responsive Education (https://crehub.org/remote-learning) Resource guide for equity and remote learning.

Equity Literacy (www.equityliteracy.org/educational-equity-resources) An extensive list of equity resources not limited to online instruction.

Equity in the Virtual Learning Classroom (www.amle.org/BrowsebyTopic/WhatsNew/WNDet/TabId/270/ArtMID/888/ArticleID/1152/Equity-in-the-Virtual-Classroom.aspx) Article from the Association of Middle Level Educators.

Equity Archives (https://onlinenetworkofeducators.org/category/online-teaching/equity/) From the Online Network of Educators, this set of materials includes all those archived under the topic of equity.

StudentsattheCenter(https://studentsatthecenterhub.org/resource/equity-resource-bundle/) Equity resources and links from the Student-Centered Learning Research Collaborative.

> Teaching Tolerance (tolerance.org) A project of the Southern Poverty Law Center, this site provides a wide range of resources, including searchable lesson plans.
> 4 Ways to Improve Digital Equity in the Classroom (www.commonsense.org/education/articles/4-ways-to-improve-digital-equity-in-your-classroom) Article that provides a solid foundation for addressing equity.

Addressing SEL Concerns

We mentioned social-emotional learning (SEL) as an equity concern earlier in this chapter. It is a concern for many students, but is a particular issue related to equity. Let's look at a model of social-emotional learning and ways you can address this issue.

A Social-Emotional Learning Model

CASEL, the Collaborative for Academic, Social, Emotional Learning, in partnership with several philanthropic foundations and Association for Supervision and Curriculum Development (ASCD), describes social-emotional learning as a process that children and adults can use to manage emotions, set and achieve positive goals, feel and show empathy for others, establish and maintain positive relationships and make responsible decisions (CASEL, 2020).

Five competencies are included in the CASEL SEL framework.

Competency	How It Manifests Itself
Self-Awareness—The ability to recognize one's emotions and thoughts and how they influence behavior.	♦ Accurately assesses own strengths and limitations ♦ Possesses a well-grounded sense of confidence and optimism
Self-Management—The ability to regulate one's emotions, thoughts and behaviors in varying situations.	♦ Able to manage stress and control impulses ♦ Capable of motivating oneself ♦ Sets and works toward achieving personal and academic goals

(Continued)

Competency	How It Manifests Itself
Social Awareness—The ability to take the perspective and empathize with others from diverse backgrounds and culture while recognizing social and ethical norms for behavior.	♦ Appreciates diversity ♦ Demonstrates respect for others ♦ Is empathetic ♦ Able to take perspective of others
Relationship Skills—The ability to establish and maintain healthy and rewarding relationships with diverse individuals and groups.	♦ Communicates clearly ♦ Good active listener ♦ Resists inappropriate social pressure ♦ Negotiates conflict constructively ♦ Seeks and offers help when needed
Responsible Decision-Making—The ability to make constructive and respectful choices about personal behavior and social interactions based on ethical standards, safety concerns, social norms and evaluation of consequences of actions.	♦ Identifies problems ♦ Analyzes solutions ♦ Evaluates actions ♦ Able to reflect on choices ♦ Acknowledges ethical responsibility

Adapted from: CASEL, Core SEL Competencies, available online at https://casel.org/core-competencies/

What Do I Do?

So, what does a principal do to assure that social-emotional learning continues to be one focus of their school's instructional program, and how does a principal support their teachers who may be questioning their own competence?

- ♦ **Assure SEL in the Curriculum**—Talk with your teachers about the importance of social-emotional learning. Discuss how the stress of a remote learning model may exacerbate issues for both students and their families. Ask teachers to identify ways to incorporate social-emotional learning into their academic program. One first-grade team in suburban Seattle set aside Friday for activities that supported their SEL curriculum.
- ♦ **Grant Permission for Flexibility and Responsiveness**—There is so much uncertainty associated with the pandemic and the school year that teachers need the flexibility

to respond to student needs as they emerge. Ask your teachers to share examples of how they monitor student SEL and respond when they identify a need.
- **Monitor Your Teachers' SEL Needs**—Throughout the book we've stressed communication and active listening. That's a key leadership skill. You should talk regularly with your teachers. We call it "checking in." During those checks, listen for indicators that your teachers are experiencing stress and shaken confidence. Respond appropriately to support them if this happens.

What If . . .

It's probably because my teachers are struggling right now, but some feel like addressing SEL with their students is just too much. They tell me they need to focus on academics.

There is a lot of pressure on teachers right now. I'd talk with them about the balance they provide in a traditional setting and they how they can adapt those strategies to remote learning. The evidence is real clear that attending to SEL actually results in better academic results. That's what I would emphasize. My guess is your school's adopted curriculum includes SEL elements. But if results is the focus, make the link between SEL and academic achievement.

- **Identify Positives and Strengths of Your Remote Program**—Often we're too busy doing things like transitioning to remote learning to recognize the good things that are happening. One of the leader's roles is to identify those things and to share the "good news" with your teachers and with your school community.
- **Advocate for Students and Teachers**—Principals often have greater access to district and community leaders. Use that access to advocate for your students and their educational needs. It may be more technology resources

or more elective options in high school. Or it might be a clearer timeline about the remainder of the school year and any potential return to face-to-face learning. And it might even be the need to assure that the school week provides teachers with adequate planning time to work on their remote learning lessons.

A Final Note

Issues about equity for students have long been a concern. These have intensified with remote learning. It's important for us to consider the issues, gather data about equity issues with our students and address the concerns, including access to technology, the Internet and other resources; scheduling; social-emotional issues; and other needs.

> ### Points to Ponder
> How does this information apply to my current situation?
> What are two to three key points to remember?
> What is one action step I would like to take?

References

Barnum, M., & Bryan, C. (2020). America's great remote-learning experiment: Surveys of teachers and parents. *eSchoolNews*. www.eschoolnews.com/2020/07/22/americas-great-remote-learning-experiment-what-surveys-of-teachers-and-parents-tell-us-about-how-it-went/

Blackburn, B. (2020). *Rigor in the remote learning classroom: Instructional tips and strategies*. Routledge.

Collaborative for Academic, Social, Emotional Learning. (2020). Core SEL competencies. *CASEL*. https://casel.org/core-competencies/

Education Trust. (2020). 10 questions for equity advocates to ask about distance learning. *Education Trust*. https://edtrust.org/resource/10-questions-for-equity-advocates-to-ask-about-distance-learning/

Williamson, R., & Blackburn, B. (2019). *Seven strategies for improving your school*. Routledge.

9

Challenges and Concerns Related to Remote Learning and Leadership

Although we have provided an overview and detailed information on a variety of key leadership activities, there are several concerns we hear from leaders.

Leadership Concerns

How do I react to a crisis?
How do I handle resistance from teachers?
How can I work with a limited budget?
How do I communicate and collaborate with parents and families?

Let's look at ways to address each issue.

How Do I React to a Crisis?

No one can predict what the rest of this school or the next will look like. Every state has its own guidelines and requirements.

As this book is published, the instructional model for many schools remains uncertain. It's unclear when instruction will return to the traditional face-to-face model, or whether it will continue remotely or be a combination of the two.

What many educators anticipate is that remote learning is not going away. It will continue to be a part of the educational landscape, and school leaders need to begin to think of it as part of the "new normal."

It's absolutely essential that school leaders continue to work with their school communities to refine and strengthen plans that can be quickly implemented if remote learning continues. As we talk with principals and teachers, we've learned that four things are essential as you do your planning.

Step 1: Engage Stakeholders

One thing is certain. A principal or other school leader can't anticipate everything that needs to be done to successfully to teach remotely. So we suggest that the first step is to engage members of your school community. Most schools already have a school improvement team or other shared decision-making group. We encourage you to convene that group to help identify the issues and plan your response. Be sure to include teachers who have experienced the first round of remote teaching.

It's also important to include parents and other family members. Make sure that every segment of your school community is represented. That includes families who may not have the same access to technology as your most affluent families and families who may be experiencing challenges in the current economy.

The key is to create a group that will engage in *open, honest discussion of the issues*, provide you with thoughtful feedback and help to chart the path forward.

Step 2: Identify the Issues and Gather Data

You've probably a long list of things to do, and you've likely identified some things that need to be improved. But we suggest that you work with the group to find out "what worked" and "what didn't work."

The path forward is clearer when you've identified any barriers and plan carefully for addressing them. In many schools distribution of technology to students and providing access to buildings to retrieve belongings are major logistical issues. Talk with your teachers and with families about how you might handle this issue in the future. There are countless other issues.

One way to gather data and insight into launching remote learning is to invite families and staff to participate in online chats. Many of us are tired of Zoom meetings, but Zoom, or another technology, provides a way to have a meaningful conversation with groups of families or with your staff.

Limit the size of the group so people can talk. Hold multiple sessions. Listen intently. Don't be critical. Not everything worked well. People understand the urgency of what happened, but they will appreciate the chance to shape future plans.

Another strategy is to conduct an online survey about your program. We encourage you to include an open-ended question where teachers and/or families can add items that may not be mentioned in the survey.

Once you've identified the issues you can get to work designing plans to address them.

Step 3: Assure a Common Base of Information

In many communities a major issue was how rapidly things changed, and access to accurate, up-to-date information was often spotty or inconsistent. Because most families balance work schedules with school and other activities, people crave information that will help them plan. So anything you can do to put in place mechanisms for up-to-date, accurate and timely information is critical to success.

Most schools have websites and use social media (Facebook, Twitter, Instagram) to share information about school activities. Make sure you have a plan for routinely updating those sites and assuring that the information that is posted is accurate. One parent described it as "a one-stop shop" for information.

Ron talked with a group of principals about communication, and they all were concerned about inaccurate posts and rumors that were spread on social media. One middle school principal said she regularly joined neighborhood social media groups like Nextdoor (https://nextdoor.com) just to "listen in" on the conversation. She said it was like "an early warning system" that alerted her to issues that were bubbling in the community and what people were talking about.

Regardless of the way you communicate, it is critical that it be monitored and managed. Monitor comments. Keep the content current and fresh. Just because the physical school is closed shouldn't mean content goes stale and is not refreshed. One principal was concerned that people reported "school was closed." He said, "We're not closed, we've just moved online."

Step 4: Anchor the Plan in Your Vision

Regardless of the plans you develop, it is critical that your school continues to align every decision with the school's shared vision. A clear, compelling vision can sustain organizations during challenges like a move to remote learning.

In addition to the school's shared vision, think about your own personal vision. What values and beliefs do you hold that should not be compromised if your school operates in a nontraditional way?

In most school communities a strong vision includes a real focus on social equity. How do you assure that every child has access to the resources for success when learning remotely? How do you support families when parents must work outside the home and aren't present to support their children's learning? How do you assure that your teachers, and other staff, have the resources needed to support students and families?

Those are critical questions, fundamental to the success of every student. But they are also issues that can be neglected in the rush to remote learning. A more intentional, deliberate plan will almost assuredly address these issues.

What If . . .

In my situation, the crisis came on quickly, was fueled by misinformation from other people and resulted in parents panicking. The best I could do was clean up the mess. What could I have done differently?

> This was a common scenario. Almost everyone, teachers, principals and particularly families, were caught off guard with the swift transition to remote learning. Hindsight is always helpful and particularly true in this case. We believe that principals should always be scanning their environment—in this case, news reports on the rising health crisis—and anticipating what may need to occur. That allows you to do some initial thinking about how to respond. It's a more active approach rather than reactive. We also think it's helpful to continuously monitor social media and other news sources to hear what misinformation may be bubbling up. It's almost like an early warning system. Monitor and then get accurate information out so that you are seen as the most accurate source of information on the issue.

How Do I Handle Resistance From Teachers?

One of the biggest challenges you may face is the resistance that emerges from teachers about remote learning. Some insist on returning to face-to-face instruction. Others demand that remote learning continue to protect the safety of students and staff. It may manifest itself through the voice of a single, highly vocal, resistant teacher or more subtly through the chatter from a small group of teachers or other staff.

Understand the Resistance

Not everyone who has concern does so because of ulterior motives. Often there is a conflict between their personal beliefs and values and the proposed changes. In one Michigan district teachers were resistant because decisions about continuing remote learning for the coming year were made in isolation by a team of school administrators. They felt that their voices were not respected and not heard, and there was inadequate consideration for the things teachers learned from the quick transition to remote learning that occurred last spring.

While some people resist just to resist, most are not that way. They are genuinely concerned about what is proposed. They either don't see the value in the change or they have concerns about how successful the change will be. With remote learning, a major consideration is student and staff safety, as well as access to quality instructional resources.

Leaders need to recognize the diverse feelings and concerns when you begin to work on any change. Individuals progress through the stages in a developmental manner. Everyone will not move at the same pace or have the same intensity of feeling.

Personal concerns about knowledge of the plans often characterize the first stage. But as you launch remote learning it's likely that significant management concerns will emerge. That can include the online platform, the balance of synchronous and asynchronous learning or online attendance problems with students. Once you're under way, teachers will become more interested in the effects of the change on students and their learning.

Handling the Toxic Teacher

Occasionally, there is one individual who resists in a way that can disrupt the entire school and detracts from the work of other teachers and staff. They're often toxic because in addition to causing disgruntlement in the workplace they spread their disgruntlement to others.

What a Leader Can Do

Here are seven steps experts recommend for managing the toxic employee (Gallo, 2016).

- **Dig Deeper**—Always take a close look at the behavior and what might be causing it. It may be because of factors outside of school or unhappiness with a colleague. Individuals and families have been affected by the pandemic in ways that are often not apparent. Another family member may have been furloughed, a relative may be hospitalized or they may be struggling with Internet access when four or five family members are online at the same time. This information may be used to coach the teacher and guide your response.

- **Provide Direct Feedback**—Toxic employees may be oblivious to their behavior and its effect on the school and other employees. Porath (2016) suggests that they may be too focused on their own needs, and it may be necessary to let them know how annoying they are. Be explicit and cite examples. Just don't dwell on it and allow them to control the conversation. Interestingly, Porath found that 4% of people engage in this kind of behavior because they think they can get away with it and they think it is just fun.
- **Explain Consequences**—Let the teacher know about the costs of their continued behavior. It may mean the need to change their schedule or assignment or even transfer or dismissal. In some states nontenured teachers can be dismissed without providing a reason.
- **Understand That Some People Don't Change**—It's always good to be optimistic and to support and encourage employees. But that doesn't work with everyone. If that's the case, you may need to talk with your human resources office about next steps.
- **Document Everything**—As with all personnel issues, be sure and document all of your conversations, your meetings and suggestions for improvement. This is particularly important if using Zoom or other video conferencing software. This helps to establish a pattern of behavior.
- **Isolate the Toxic Person and "Immunize" the Team**—If the toxic behavior persists and the person remains in your school, you can isolate them and minimize their impact. You can change their assignment, schedule fewer meetings and lessen the contact with colleagues. If other employees come to you about their toxic colleague, hold one-on-one conversations but be discrete and coach them on how to minimize contact and interaction.
- **Don't Get Distracted**—Finally, a toxic teacher has a way of consuming your time and energy. Don't allow that to happen. Find time to counteract their behavior by working and interacting with employees who are supportive

and engaged. And, of course, take care of your own work–life balance, something discussed earlier in this chapter.

Focus on Students

It seems so obvious to always think about students first. But we've found that when complex and difficult issues arise, student interests are often secondary to the interests of teachers, parents or the community. Part of the problem is that everything that people want to do is always described as being "in the best interests of students." Often diametrically opposed ideas are described that way.

William Roberts, principal of Los Altos High School in Hacienda Heights, California, talked with Ron about how he handled challenging teachers. He said that he always asked his staff, "How would you want your child to be treated? What would you want their program to be like?" He found that for many of his teachers those questions forced them to consider the needs of their students through their perspective as a parent. It changed the conversation.

How Can I Work With a Limited Budget?

No school is immune from the need to adjust their budget in response to the pandemic and remote learning. Schools are caught between expectations for quality instructional programs and the reality that there may be fewer human and financial resources to support the program. At the same time there is almost a universal need for improved technology, enhanced curricular and instructional software including a platform for delivery of the program, and expenses related to safety and cleaning as you prepare for the return to a face-to-face program. Almost universally, the issue is one of how to be both efficient and more effective.

The Four "Rs" of Resource Management

Most schools have learned that reducing every program a little isn't very effective. You simply can't use that approach to find the resources you will need to reallocate. It may be necessary to focus on fewer things and do them really well.

What's clear is that everything must be on the table—the way a school uses technology, time, space, instructional materials and personnel. Protecting learning opportunities for children must always be the highest priority. Especially important is that the voices of children and families *most in need* be heard in all of our decision-making processes.

Four approaches to managing the budget have been identified, the "Four Rs"—Reduce, Refine, Reprioritize and Regenerate (Johnston & Williamson, 2014).

Many of these approaches are not easy and may not be enthusiastically embraced by staff, parents, students or even community leaders. But they are most successful when made in a collaborative and inclusive environment, one that welcomes open debate and values consensus building. The dilemma for many schools is that the move to remote learning occurred quickly, demanding rapid decisions and allowing little time for discussion or deliberation.

1. Reduce

Reductions are often the most common response to declining resources. If necessary, cuts should be made in a fair, reasonable, transparent and humane manner. Reducing the budget most often involves freezing current spending, making across-the-board cuts, identifying targeted reductions or eliminating programs.

Reducing budgets is something no one likes, but almost everyone understands. What people want is information about the impact it will have on them, their programs or their children. We believe good fiscal decision-making has several elements that you should use when making choices to reduce the budget.

- **Provide High-Quality Information**—Help people understand the problem, steps taken to soften the effect and the data used to make decisions.
- **Have a Consistent Message**—People rely on those they trust (including social media friends) for information and

not necessarily school leaders. Invest in "internal public relations" to make sure everyone in the school has the same information and the same message about reductions or reallocations.
- **Maintain Confidentiality**—Be careful what you say and to whom you say it. If reductions target a program or specific personnel, don't let a leak reveal the information first.
- **Address Key Issues Directly**—Deal with real concerns as soon as possible. Everyone wants to know if they will lose their job. Make sure messages are accurate and lessen rumors and anxiety.
- **Don't Make Promises**—Statements made early can feel like a commitment, and trust will be damaged if your "promise" can't be kept.
- **Value Dissent**—Recognize that dissenting opinions are always uncomfortable but important. They can reveal problems that weren't thought about, and they can give you clues about the resistance you may encounter.

2. Refine

Schools can also reorganize, streamline or improve efficiency without cutting programs. The focus is finding the most efficient way to achieve goals rather than making a fundamental change. The Annenberg Institute for School Reform (Barnes, 2004) suggests four areas where refinements work best—human resource use and development, school organization, fiscal and technical resources and social resources.

- **Human Resource Use and Development**—There are several general strategies that you can consider to refine the human resource mix in your school (Petrilli, 2012).
    - Ask teachers to take on additional responsibilities for additional pay rather than hire additional staff.
    - Reduce ancillary positions or specialized personnel.
    - Trade down by getting services for lower cost. For example, use county health personnel rather than

school nurses, or partner with the local library rather than hire media specialists.
- Invest in staff by cross-training so teachers can teach in more than one area.
- **School Organization**—Take a look at how your school is organized. Increasing social distancing and reducing class size will affect staffing. An elementary school in Mukilteo, Washington, reallocated a physical education teacher, a music teacher and an art teacher to general classroom positions in order to meet reduced class size goals.
- **Fiscal and Technical Resources**—Spend money on things that work and stop spending money on things that don't. That may require a tough examination of past practices and a willingness to abandon things that have been in place for a long time. Assure that your technology strengthens and enhances the program. Some schools teach foreign language using Rosetta Stone or some other online software system rather than a traditional classroom. Or arrange online tutoring from low-cost college students, retirees or volunteers to supplement your classroom teachers.
- **Social Resources**—Community assets are a tremendous resource. Partnerships are ways of using community assets to increase your resources. Think about potential partners in your community and devote time to cultivating relationships that can benefit your school.

3. Reprioritize School Goals

This is perhaps the most complex of the four strategies because of the need to think deeply about the school's mission and values and which activities are most closely aligned with the mission. Rather than tinkering with programs, reprioritizing reconsiders whether to maintain programs that don't align with the school's mission. While an important strategy, reprioritizing can be a challenge when moving quickly to a remote program.

There is no single process that makes reprioritizing easy. Rethinking some of a school's fundamental operations can lead to new priorities. In many districts that has included thinking about a four-day week, even greater use of technology including continuing online options for parents after the pandemic and online professional development. Other funding from local, state or federal grants may help pay for some programs or services.

When reprioritizing, it is important to use a process that is inclusive of all interest groups, that is focused on building consensus and that values disparate points of view.

4. Regenerate

Generating additional resources or finding new sources of funds can support the move to remote learning. Additional funding can come from business or community partnerships, school foundations, grants, fees and entrepreneurial activity.

- **Business Partnerships**—Many local businesses have an interest in supporting the local schools. They may be able to provide support for specific programs. Quicken Loans, a Detroit-based company, funded procurement of tablet devices for distribution to students. A restaurant group in suburban Seattle provided sandwiches and other food to supplement the elementary school lunch program in several districts. They are most successful when there is a mutually supportive relationship and the partners commit themselves to specific goals and activities clearly linked to benefiting students. While additional resources are good for a school, they are also good for a business that may have enhanced goodwill and a stronger presence in the community.
- **Community Partnerships**—Community partnerships bring together the resources of local businesses, service clubs, nonprofit agencies, volunteers, churches, colleges and universities—almost anyone with an interest in children and young people. They are a powerful social resource that schools can tap into to support their educational programs. One service club in the Columbus,

Ohio, area provided technical support to help families resolve problems with Internet access.

- **School Foundations**—Many schools and school districts create their own foundations to support educational programs. Many of those foundations are reallocating their resources to support school needs when they move to remote learning.
- **Grants and Entrepreneurial Activity**—You can become much more aggressive in seeking grants and contracts. This is a more long-term approach but can often secure funding for innovative programs, especially those involving technology. A consortium of five small Oregon districts shared the costs of a grant writer and by the end of the first year found that the new grants justified the grant writing expense.

How Can We Communicate and Collaborate With Parents?

Partnering with the parents and families of your students provides advantages to you, your students and their families. Families will have a better idea of what's happening in school, which also allows them to help support their son or daughter at home. Students benefit when they receive encouragement at home. And teachers and leaders benefit when learning is reinforced and supported by parents and families.

Communicating and working with parents and families is a particular challenge in a remote learning setting. It's still our responsibility to connect with parents, and the benefits outweigh any costs in terms of time. There are three ways to partner with parents.

> Connect.
> Inform.
> Encourage.

Connect

Many parent and family partnerships are destroyed before they start because the teacher believes it is someone else's responsibility to prompt a connection. This was exactly the attitude of my former colleague, who told me, "If a parent doesn't contact you that is great. Just lay low and you'll be able to do what you want." If you believe it's the responsibility of parents and families to communicate and/or follow up with you, that attitude comes through when you talk with them. Connecting with parents is not an extra job; it is part of your job. There is no way you can truly help your students be successful without the support of their parents.

Connecting With Parents

Learn their names.
Always begin with a positive comment.
Avoid blame.
Share good news regularly.
Ask them to help you understand their son or daughter.
Ask for input with selected decisions.
Hold virtual open houses.
Hold virtual teacher conferences.

One particular activity we like is a vision letter. Ideally completed at the start of the year, you ask parents and family members to write you a letter. In the letter, they imagine it is the end of the school year and it was the best school year ever for their child, grandchild, niece, nephew, etc. They look "back" on the year and describe for you what happened. What did they think went well, what did the student learn, or why did their student thrive? They are able to be as detailed as they would like and can write the letter, provide a video or use any format they prefer. When you read the letter, you may be surprised at what you learn. We've found families have never been asked their point of view on what would make a successful school year, and they are happy to share. In many cases, I've heard parents share how honored they were that a teacher or leader would want to know what they think.

For many families it is a hectic time juggling their own work schedules and their children's remote learning. School leaders often use video to get out messages directly to families. Rather than send an email, send a short self-recorded video updating families on your remote learning plan. Keep the videos short but make them informative and useful.

Inform

Next, keep your students' parents and families informed. Too often, problems occur when there is a misunderstanding. You'll want to communicate detailed information at the start of the year, then provide ongoing material throughout the year. How much? That depends on your situation, the parents and families and your students.

What types of information should you share? That is typically determined by what you want to accomplish. Some parents need more detailed information; others need very little. As we talked with parents who were adjusting to the new "remote reality" from COVID-19, they shared a variety of comments.

> I'd like to know how to prioritize if we don't have time to do everything.
> What is the best way for me to help my child?
> How do I know I am doing the right things?
> How will I know if my son or daughter is successful?

As you read their comments, you are probably thinking about information you should provide. One of the goals of parent communication is to provide details about the most critical aspects of remote learning. There is standard information parents and families need, such as contact information for the school district, local schools and IT support. They will also need to know how to contact you and your teachers, as well as your office hours.

Distribute the information widely, using traditional and social media formats so that families are familiar with it. Always publish the information in major languages spoken by students and their families. You'll also want to give them general information that will be helpful throughout the year.

General Tips for Parents

Encourage your son or daughter to give 100% at all times but understand when the stress is simply too much for him or her and it's time for a break.

Reinforce concepts and habits the teacher is trying to build. If Jonathan is learning how to multiply percentages, have him help you calculate the sales tax of a grocery or online order.

If possible, create a designated quiet, well-lit environment at home with all of the materials necessary for completing school tasks (extra paper, scissors, pens, pencils, pencil sharpener, a dictionary, markers, highlighters, a ruler, calculator, index cards, etc.).

Prevent brain freeze—allow your son or daughter to take a short break every 30 minutes or between tasks. Taking time to move around during that break is beneficial. It's also okay to take longer breaks periodically if needed.

Be careful not to give answers; instead, offer advice about where to look for an answer.

Follow the schedule and guidelines provided by the teacher. If you need to, ask the teacher for help prioritizing tasks for your son or daughter.

In addition to providing general tips for parents, you might consider creating information sheets about key topics related to your specific content. Develop clear, step-by-step instructions on the use of your platform and the online tools used most often by students. Many students will be adept at their use, but others will struggle. Many districts have a location on the first page of their school's website that links to the instructions or short video tutorials. You can distribute them via your school's website, through social media or in paper format. Always include how to connect with someone for additional technical support if needed.

> **Sample Topical Tip Sheets**
> Problem-Solving in Math.
> How to Read Online.
> Searching for Information Online.
> Participating in Zoom (or other appropriate technology tools).

Another option is a virtual family academy. Schools have long hosted parent events designed to share information with families. They've adapted this strategy during remote learning and host online events like "Digital Parenting 101" designed to educate parents on the platform, apps and online system. Another district held a parent academy about using the mandatory EdTech tools their children would be using. You can record the meetings and make them available online for parents who are unable to participate. You can post the videos on easy-to-use platforms like YouTube.

Encourage

Encouraging parents and families is also a critical part of building a relationship, and it is especially important during remote learning. Most of the parents we spoke with said they needed even more encouragement during remote learning. See if you have heard any of these comments.

> **Parents' Comments**
> How do I get started?
> I'm not sure if I'm doing the right things.
> I am overwhelmed! I don't know what to do next.
> How do I know what is most important?

Providing information responds to some concerns, but just as students need encouragement, so do their parents and families. Some parents are working at home and trying to help their sons and daughters; some are working and cannot help until the workday ends; and some have multiple children and are just overwhelmed. And, just like students, some need more encouragement than others. As you build relationships and communicate regularly, you will know when and how to encourage parents and families. Much of your encouragement will be comments that praise what they are doing well, as well as sharing suggestions in a supportive manner. Your words and any nonverbal cues will make a difference to them. You can use video messages, chats, emails, phone calls, social media or "snail mail" for encouragement.

Although we've discussed providing information to parents and families, there are times that ongoing information can be encouraging. For example, the video "A Parent's Guide to At-Home Learning" (https://youtu.be/p9CdQFnt79I) is a motivating boost for families.

What If . . .

These are great tips, but how do I handle a resistant parent or family? I've tried everything, and I am just frustrated.

> *Start by recognizing that some families are just not going to be happy with remote learning. Let's be honest: remote learning leans heavily on parents to help with the education of their children, disrupts routines and may affect parents' work schedules. Not every family has the resources to provide daycare or to acquire all the technology and other materials (think desks) that might be needed. Be careful not to label it "resistance" when it might be other issues. Check with the child's teacher to see if they have insights that might be helpful. If you've talked with the family, listened carefully to their concerns and if they're still unhappy, give yourself credit for what you've done. Talk with a colleague about additional options. Sometimes we just have to acknowledge that there are people who will continue to resist.*

A Final Note

You will face specific challenges as you lead change in a remote learning setting. Knowing how to react to situations, support your personnel, deal with negativity, manage your budget and communicate with parents and families will support your efforts.

Points to Ponder

How does this information apply to my current situation?
What are two to three key points to remember?
What is one action step I would like to take?

References

Barnes, F. (2004). *Inquiry and action: Making school improvement part of daily practice.* Annenberg Institute for School Reform at Brown University.
Blackburn, B. (2020). *Rigor in the remote learning classroom: Instructional tips and strategies.* Routledge.
Gallo, A. (2016). How to manage a toxic employee. *Harvard Business Review.* https://hbr.org/2016/10/how-to-manage-a-toxic-employee
Johnston, J. H., & Williamson, R. (2014). *Leading schools in an era of declining resources.* Routledge.
Petrilli, M. (2012). *How districts can stretch the school dollar.* Fordham Institute.
Porath, C. (2016). *Mastering civility: A manifesto for the workplace.* Grand Central Publishing.
Williamson, R., & Blackburn, B. (2019). *Seven strategies for improving your school.* Routledge.
Williamson, R., & Johnston, J. H. (2012). *The school leader's guide to social media.* Routledge.

10

Focusing on Yourself as a Leader in a Remote Environment

Few jobs are as complex and involve as many different responsibilities as the school principalship. Managing them can, at times, seem overwhelming, and principals often find themselves caught up in necessary but less important tasks.

Ron's son-in-law is an elementary school principal in suburban Seattle that has moved to remote learning. He says his friends frequently ask what he's doing now that schools are closed. But, in fact, he's never been busier. The traditional tasks remain, although slightly altered. In addition, a whole new set of tasks emerged. There may be a hyper-emphasis on communication, a learning curve around safety protocols, numerous parent concerns about rigor of the curriculum and access to technology, along with the need to support teachers in their switch to online or remote learning.

It's hard for the public to understand that a principal's work continues even when remote learning is occurring. Managing the tasks is important because principals want to be seen as "staying on top" of things. Their reputation, and that of their school, is often directly linked to their ability to juggle multiple priorities and accomplish multiple tasks at the same time.

> **Key Areas**
>
> Manage your time.
> Maintain work–life balance.
> Learn continuously.
> Avoid decision fatigue.
> Manage the unexpected.
> Manage privacy.

Manage Your Time

A recent study found that when working remotely, the boundaries between work and personal lives became clouded (McGregor, 2020). Employees often worked longer hours and were expected to attend more online meetings because there weren't the normal cues about the end of the workday like the end of the school day or the need to drive home for dinner. That's created an almost universal recognition that managing time, and managing the boundaries between work and personal lives, is an essential skill for those working remotely.

Despite the almost universal recognition that leaders need to manage their time wisely, there is little research on practices that are most effective. What is known is that how you manage time affects job performance, your stress level and your personal life (Claessens et al., 2007).

Time management consists of three behaviors: setting goals and priorities, the mechanics of organizing and doing one's job and each individual's unique style and preferences (Macan, 1994). In other words, what works for one leader may not be useful for another. This recognition of the idiosyncratic nature of time management means there are all sorts of strategies to effective time management. The most effective approach is the one that works best for an individual leader.

While the research on time management is meager, all sorts of time management tools and strategies emerge from the literature. These strategies generally include developing a clear set of priorities, organizing your tasks and identifying specific techniques to complete those tasks.

Step 1: Assess Where You Are and How You Spend Time

It's likely that you need to rebalance the use of time as a result of the new responsibilities associated with remote learning.

Virtually all recommendations about time management suggest beginning with an assessment of your work and priorities. The first step is to recognize the strengths and challenges of your current time management. Clarifying where you are is an important step in beginning to change your situation. Take a few minutes and assess your current situation.

Strengths	Challenges

The list of challenges, while often long, is most often not nearly as out of control as may be thought. Taking time to assess the current situation is often helpful in gaining "a dose of reality" and control about your situation.

Next, identify your most important, or essential, responsibilities. Then describe the tasks associated with those responsibilities. Covey (1996) describes these as the "big rocks" and suggests in *First Things First* that these tasks must always be taken care of first before the other smaller and less important tasks. These top priorities must be scheduled, or they will be neglected. For principals, they are the "big rocks" that most often drive student learning. While every school is a little different, those priorities generally revolve around improving instruction and student learning.

Think about your remote learning program. What are the essential tasks that must be attended to in order to assure a quality educational program for your students? Now create a vision of how you want to spend your time. Imagine a day in which you are relaxed and productive. For example, if your work were completely effective, efficient and balanced, how would you spend your time?

Here are some strategies that can help with this task:

- Select a week and use a journal to record how you spend time. This will help you identify how much you can get done and identify the most useful time, as well as the most unproductive, or distracting, time.
- Take the first 30 minutes of every day to plan your day. Don't start until the plan is completed. This activity helps focus the day and what you want to accomplish.
- Before every scheduled call or meeting, take a couple of minutes and clarify what you want to accomplish. It helps to identify what success looks like during the call or meeting. Similarly, take five minutes following every call or meeting to reflect and determine if you achieved the results you desired and to clarify next steps.
- Think about patterns in your day. For example, the beginning of the day can be an important time to connect with teachers and students. How will you continue those connections while working remotely? What other patterns during the day need to be addressed? Anticipate those patterns and allot time for these visits.
- If unannounced calls or texts arrive, think about how you will manage them. Develop a system for monitoring and responding to unexpected requests.

Step 2: Make a Mental Adjustment

Many principals feel overwhelmed with the responsibilities of their role. Our thoughts drive our feelings and actions. We've found it helpful if we want to make a change to start with an adjustment in how we think about what we are doing.

From Negative Thought	*To Positive Thought*
I'll never be able to keep up with teachers' messages.	I'm replying to teachers in a timely manner every day.
I'll never be able to manage everything remotely.	I will adapt what works for me when we are all in the physical school in order to manage things remotely.
It's impossible to keep everybody happy.	Every interaction I have with people will be sincere regardless of their behavior.

Focus on the positive progress you make each day, whether it is effectively delegating a task or responding to a teacher's need for additional support with technology. Give credit to others, and to yourself, for the things you accomplish each day. One principal told Ron he always ended the day making a list of the things that were accomplished and creating a list of things to focus on the next day.

What If . . .

I've been working on focusing on positive aspects of my job. But the rest of my leadership team isn't on board. No matter what I say or do, they concentrate on what is wrong.

First, don't change your behavior. Continue to focus on the positive. You may want to meet individually with other members of your team and talk with them about how things are going. Don't be accusatory. We find that people often talk differently when in a one-on-one conversation than they do in a group. If you hear negativity, then you may want identify things they are doing that are positive and share those with them. But stay the course and continue to focus on the positive.

Control Self-Interruption—There are lots of ways to distract yourself from what needs to be done. Distraction is most likely to occur when the task is unpleasant or requires energy or skills you lack at that moment. Distraction may come from the organization of the office or your workspace if working from home. Materials needed for a task should be organized and easily accessible. That can be a major problem if working remotely. If the interruption is mental fatigue, move around and stretch, take a short walk, eat a healthy snack or meditate for a few minutes. Some principals actually schedule time for high-priority work.

Do, Delegate or Delete—A critical mental adjustment is to recognize that every task doesn't require the principal to complete it. Think about the daily routine and consider what may detract from your productivity. Identify the tasks that you really must do, those that can be delegated to someone else and those that don't need to be done. This critical assessment often identifies nonessential tasks that detract from accomplishing the most essential tasks.

Only Handle It Once (OHIO)—One of the most prevalent time management suggestions is to read an email, memo or message only once. Reading them multiple times multiplies the time you spend. It's more efficient to take a minute and decide what to do and move it out of your inbox or off your desk. The only exception should be tasks that are delegated to another person.

Just Say No—One of the hardest things for many leaders to do is to say no. Leaders worry that people's feelings will be hurt or they will lose support (Haden, 2015). Four questions help you master the art of saying no:

- Am I capable and qualified to do what's being asked?
- Do I have time for this task or activity?
- Do I want to do this activity?
- What are the ramifications of saying no?

Everything Is Not An Emergency—Remember that most emergencies are only in the eye of the beholder. Not every problem is a crisis, particularly if the problem resulted from someone else's poor planning. Of course, authentic emergencies occur and you must respond, but in many cases so-called emergencies do not require immediate attention. Work toward minimizing urgent tasks.

Take Care of Yourself—It's an old adage, but caregivers need to take care of themselves so that they can care for others. School leaders are important caregivers, especially when there's an abrupt change to school operations like moving to remote learning.

School leaders are expected to stay up-to-date on the latest information affecting students and their learning, and with remote learning, that information suddenly changed. With the arrival of the pandemic, a whole new set of responsibilities arose. Among them are issues with access to technology, supporting teachers who are teaching remotely for the first time, learning about safety protocols for students and staff, the need for increased communication with families and planning for both remote learning and the eventual return to face-to-face instruction.

Too often, the demands of the job mean that little time is available to devote to your own professional learning. As we all learned this past year, it's hard to predict the future. But what we know is that schools, and their leaders, will continue to be buffeted by a whole set of issues, the least of which is the switch to remote learning.

Every principal knows that change is part of the job. But change can be difficult, particularly when it occurs suddenly and with little advance notice. It often requires changing old habits and adjusting perspectives, and an even more complex workload. But there are other needs as well, like the balance between work and your personal life or dealing with some of the challenges that come from a transition to remote learning.

Because the principalship is a demanding job, it is important that principals invest in their own health, their personal relationships and their interests and avocations. Almost all principals are exhausted at the end of the day, and good time management includes finding time for yourself and managing your own physical, emotional, mental and spiritual resources. The very best, most effective caregivers are those that pay attention to their own needs and take care of their own physical and emotional health. Here are some common-sense suggestions (Marshall, 2008).

- Exercise faithfully (three times a week recommended).
- Eat the right foods, starting with a healthy breakfast.
- Get enough sleep.
- Carve out time for relaxation and fun.
- Build a support system of friends, mentors and significant others.
- Orchestrate small and large wins to provide an extra shot of optimism and energy. Be comfortable rewarding yourself.

Step 3: Create or Identify Structures to Support Your Plan

The third step in good time management is to create a set of regular, consistent structures that will support a productive day. There is no one perfect strategy—except the one that works for you. However, there are several strategies that other principals have found effective.

Here are other ideas worthy of consideration.

Use a Journal—Several principals we know maintain a running journal, either electronic or on paper, to take notes from meetings, calls and emails and create a "to do" list. This ensures that everything is in one place rather than on multiple pieces of paper or multiple sticky notes. A journal also makes it easy to look back and find ideas and tasks that emerged at earlier meetings

Maintain a Single Calendar—Nothing can be more confusing and lead to missed commitments than the use of multiple calendars. An Oregon principal puts tasks she wants to accomplish on her calendar as a reminder. Synching electronic calendars to computers that maintain your calendar should be a daily function.

Take Control of Email/Texts—Managing email or texts can be a major time management issue. Check them at set times, not all the time. Morgenstern (2005) encourages managers to not check it before 10:00 a.m. She suggests that checking email first thing each day allows the email to set the day's agenda. Rather than responding to email, she encouraged using the first two hours of each day to work on your most important priorities rather than acting on the most recent request. Turn off the automatic notification of your email or instant messaging (IM) program. When it beeps, it distracts you from your work.

Establish Norms Around Access—When working in a remote environment, it can feel like everyone has access all the time. The number of emails and texts can be overwhelming. While everyone wants to be responsive, a literal open door can lead to fragmentation of your day. Identify a quiet time each day to respond to email. Don't reinforce the idea that you respond the moment you receive a message. Establish norms around interruptions. Access is important, but uninterrupted time to accomplish tasks is also important. Consider setting blocks of time when you will not be interrupted except in emergencies.

Schedule a "To Do Meeting"—Schedule a short, regular meeting with your leadership team to review key activities and delegate items to others in the team. You may do this through regular written communication instead of a meeting.

Maintain Work–Life Balance

Finding the balance between personal and professional responsibilities is a struggle for many school leaders. The job is complex. The day is long and filled with expectations from both senior leadership in the district and from families and the community (Whitaker, 1996). The idea that school leaders are available any time, any day of the week adds stress, especially with the ready access to technology.

While the importance of work–life balance is well documented, there is no single strategy or approach that works for everyone. Balance, in the truest sense of the word, is not about compartmentalizing your life. As David Allen in *Getting Things Done* (2015) notes, it's about being appropriately engaged with what you are doing in the moment.

The Importance of Balance

Work–life balance doesn't necessarily mean there is an equal division between the two. Individual interests, goals, obligations and commitments mean that the balance is more fluid and shifts over time. But the evidence is clear that work–life balance positively affects individuals as well as the organizations where they work. Here's a summary of the benefits.

Benefits for the Individual	*Benefits for the School*
♦ Work–life balance contributes to a healthier life. ♦ Stress is reduced when there is balance. ♦ Relationships improve both on the job and away from the job. ♦ Your work, as well as your personal life, is more satisfying.	♦ There is increased productivity and commitment at work. ♦ Teamwork and communication are improved. ♦ Overall organizational stress is reduced. ♦ The collective morale improves.

Four big strategies can help you improve the balance in your life.

> **Four Strategies to Achieve Balance**
> 1. Assess where you are and where you want to be.
> 2. Set realistic goals and expectations.
> 3. Create structures to manage your work–life balance.
> 4. Communicate, communicate, communicate.

Assess Your Current Work–Life Balance

The first step is to recognize the strengths and challenges you face. One principal we interviewed was so overwhelmed, she said, "I don't think I can make a list. It will make it seem worse!" That's not true. You may think you don't have time for this step, or you may not want to think about all the challenges, but it is critical in order to make progress.

In order to achieve work–life balance you need to think about yourself, the patterns in your life and your aspirations. Here are some suggestions for assessing where you are and where you want to be.

Define what "greater balance" means for you, and think about what you value. Being clear about your values is one key to establishing balance, or at least understanding why you don't have balance. A conflict in values can create stress and disrupt the balance we seek. For example, you may value time with your spouse, children or significant other before your day begins but you find yourself at your computer responding to messages from the moment you wake up. Perhaps you value responding to your staff, but also value attending your childrens' activities or being available to help with childcare or household chores while your partner works remotely.

Plan for Greater Balance

Next, identify patterns in your daily routine and understand your natural workday rhythms. Think about how you prefer to organize your day. What things always get accomplished and what things get deferred? What choices do you make about sleep, diet and exercise? Do you prefer to get started early, or do you reserve that time for transitioning from personal to work? People have their own natural rhythms. Identify your rhythms and patterns during the day. Pay attention to your patterns over the day, assuring adequate breaks and time to rejuvenate. Then plan your day based on your patterns and rhythms.

Set Realistic Goals and Expectations

Finding work–life balance is about setting priorities and managing time (Graham, 2002; Uscher, 2011). Our perceptions, attitudes and assumptions shape the expectations we have for ourselves. Here are some suggestions for setting realistic goals.

Tips for Setting Realistic Goals

- *Check out assumptions about your work.* Talk with your supervisor about priorities and balance. Often we set unrealistic standards for our own performance. When working remotely, it's easy to be pulled into a 24/7 workday. Good supervisors know the importance of work–life balance and how a lack of balance can negatively affect an individual's work and the entire organization (Chakravarty, 2011).
- *Talk with your family or significant other* about priorities and schedules. Much of the stress about work–life balance is a result of tension with those we care about the most. Talking about the issues and being open to finding solutions help lessen the stress (Graham, 2002).
- *Include time for yourself* and your own personal interests as one of your goals. Be sure to allow time for adequate sleep and exercise. Make healthy choices about what, and when, you eat (Anderson, 2013).

Communicate, Communicate, Communicate

While planning is helpful to work–life balance, even more helpful is communication with your supervisor and with your spouse or significant other. In the absence of communication others are left to form their own opinions and make their own judgments. Here are some other communication tips from the University of Maine (Graham, 2002).

> ***Tips for Communication***
> - Hold family meetings to talk about schedules and priorities. The schedule can be incredibly complex when everyone is working or learning remotely.
> - Keep both weekly and monthly schedules that include time for your priorities, including exercise, family activities and personal interests.
> - Be willing to revise your plans when there are conflicts or change is needed.
> - Understand what you can control and what you can't.
> - Keep a sense of humor.
> - Remember that effective work–life balance is not a static event, developed one time, but a process that evolves and changes over time.

Learn Continuously

The shift to remote learning reinforced the importance of continuous learning. We learned that change will occur and often at an accelerating pace. In fact, at times in recent months it's felt like the guidance on student safety or on online platforms changed daily. As a principal, how will you respond to change that you do not control? Or how can you anticipate change when change is around every corner? There are eight strategies you can use to learn and be able to respond.

1. Analyze your environment: Scan the environment in which your school exists—district, community, state,

nation and world. Identify issues that affect your organization and those that affect the world more broadly. These trends and issues often emerge as important. What do you need to learn about these trends? Where can you gather that information?

2. Monitor changes in the environment: Read voraciously, talk with a broad selection of people in your community and stay current with trends at the state and national level.

3. Identify the factors needed for success: Look beyond the traditional educational factors (good teachers, more money) and consider issues that emerged more recently, like assuring every student has access to robust Internet access or that teachers have the training they need to provide quality online instruction. If possible, connect with leaders outside of education and learn how they respond to these challenges.

4. Think about your own assumptions: After identifying some of the assumptions you hold about your school and its environment, test those by assessing their degree of certainty (high, medium, low) and the level of impact (high, medium, low). Assumptions play an important role in constructing the future, and they should be as reliable as possible. For example, some educators are surprised that over half of families prefer a remote learning program to traditional face-to-face instruction. What does that mean when it's possible to return to traditional face-to-face instruction?

5. Consider an alternative future: Consider the issues you think will have an impact on your school and the factors you identified that are critical to success. Will families continue to trust schools as safe places for their children? Will schools need to continue to provide families with a remote learning alternative? How do I develop the technological capacity of my teachers and other staff?

6. Think about the alternatives: Consider every option to identify the most likely. Begin to think about how you, your staff and your school district will respond to this

new reality. Use technology to test the alternatives with other principals, leaders in other fields and those in your professional network.
7. Develop plans for needed action: Identify steps that can be taken to respond to the anticipated future. "Hedging strategies" can help cope with undesirable futures. "Shaping strategies" can help create the desired future. Regardless, you should anticipate what might occur and begin to develop contingency plans for dealing with those possibilities.
8. Implement plans and monitor progress: Launch initiatives to create the desired future and gather data about progress. Use these data to continue the process by scanning the environment and planning for the future.

Although it is impossible to predict the future, it is possible to anticipate the trends and issues that will affect your school.

What Do I Do?

Every year we work with dozens of principals, and we've come to appreciate the challenges they face. Principals are asked to solve some of the most complex and contentious issues in schooling, and over the past few months many have been tasked with moving their school to a totally remote or hybrid learning model. We marvel at their energy and their capacity for change. From these principals, we've learned things you can do to continue your own learning.

Be a Continuous Learner

◆ Be intellectually curious. Read a lot and think a lot about current and emerging trends. Be open to ways to improve your school even when things are going well. There is a lot of information online about how schools responded to remote learning. Spend time

with traditional publications and online, in education and in other fields, to learn about trends and new ideas and to promote your own thinking.
- Cultivate a critical friend, someone outside your school or outside education. Such a friend can provide a fresh perspective on issues you face.
- Actively participate in every professional development activity with your teachers. Value the opportunity to learn from them, to reflect on your learning and to apply it in your work.
- Talk with others about what you read, what you've watched and what you've learned. Sharing your learning models the importance of learning. You might share something you've learned at the beginning of a staff or team meeting.
- Organize a discussion group with other principals. Identify a shared interest or select a book of interest and commit to sharing your thinking and ideas. Zoom or other online platforms can provide a structure for online book study.
- Join the online communities of your professional association (NAESP, NASSP, ASCD) and tap into the advice they provide.
- Enjoy what you do. Relish the impact that principals have on the education of students in their school. When the enjoyment fades, find ways to reinvigorate your passion and model the importance of continuous learning.

The good news is that technology has made staying connected far easier than it has ever been. Use some of the online options mentioned earlier, or simply use your computer's search engine to find an abundance of information about the experience of other schools in the move to remote learning.

What If...

I have always believed in lifelong learning, but I'm struggling right now. I still believe I need to focus on my own learning, but there just isn't time. I'm so overwhelmed that my own learning needs are taking a back seat right now.

It's been a challenging time for principals. Some things are more important than others, and you need to be clear about those. The switch to remote learning changed routines, disrupted lives and required a whole new set of skills like managing technology and implementing safety protocols. At the same time you were expected to simultaneously plan and launch a remote learning program, which we suspect was learning, just not the kind you might have selected on your own. Be sure to review our suggestions about time management. Then, when the crisis has passed, be sure to get back to being a continual learner.

Avoid Decision Fatigue

Have you ever noticed how later in the day it gets tougher to make a decision or even more challenging to pick an option from among those presented? It's not uncommon to face this dilemma in both our personal and professional lives. It's a concept called decision fatigue, and psychologists and others have begun to recognize how it affects the decisions we make.

School leaders, who hold some of the most complicated jobs in our society, are routinely asked to make decisions, both important and unimportant, complicated and less so, throughout the day. The sheer variety of issues faced by school leaders and the rapid pace at which they are asked to make decisions mean that those leaders must remain focused and have the mental energy for sound decision-making.

But decision fatigue affects more than just one's professional life. After a long day at work, decision fatigue may affect your personal life. Ever notice how difficult it can be to decide where to go for dinner, or even what to serve? It's just one more decision among many you're asked to make and it can be one too many.

What Is Decision Fatigue?

Decision fatigue is a term that describes the deterioration in the quality of decisions made by people, particularly later in the day and after making several routine or complex decisions. It acknowledges that during the day a person may deplete their mental energy, thus affecting their ability to make rational decisions, and can result in poorer decisions later in the day.

Decision fatigue can cloud one's judgment, leading to poor choices. It explains a whole set of undesirable behaviors such as losing focus in meetings, getting angry with colleagues, being impulsive or even making irrational decisions without considering the consequences (Green, 2011).

Implications of Decision Fatigue

When one experiences decision fatigue, they often don't feel physically tired, so one is not aware that fatigue is occurring. But declining mental energy has several implications for leaders, and several effects of decision fatigue have been identified.

> **Reduced Ability to Make a Choice**—Decisions where options exist can be energy-consuming as the decision maker analyzes both the benefits and costs of each option. People with depleted energy may become reluctant to make trade-offs or they may make poor decisions.
> **Decision Paralysis**—Decision fatigue can also lead decision makers to simply not make decisions.
> **Impulse Decisions**—Decision fatigue has also been connected to impulsive decisions. Later in the day, the brain looks for shortcuts and acts impulsively rather than expending even more energy to make a decision.
> **Impaired Self-Regulation**—There is some evidence that decision-making may drain some of a person's internal resources, leaving them less capable of handling other activities, including in their private lives.

Strategies to Minimize Decision Fatigue

The good news is that while decision fatigue cannot be avoided, researchers have also identified several strategies for minimizing the effects.

- **Recognize It Is a Problem**—First, don't minimize the problem or believe that you are immune to the effects. Monitor your behavior and the decisions you make and plan accordingly.
- **Plan Your Day**—Once you recognize the effect of decision fatigue, schedule your day so that important meetings or decisions occur early in the day. An alternative is to schedule that Zoom meeting or make the decision following lunch or a midday break. Basically, make your most important decisions in the morning.
- **Avoid Back-to-Back Meetings**—Avoid the tendency to schedule consecutive meetings, especially online. Take a break between meetings so that you can have a short break and recharge your mental energy reserves. Use the time between meetings to get up, move around and do things that do not require complex decision-making.
- **Take Short Mental Breaks**—As noted earlier, recognize the importance of taking breaks and actually schedule them throughout the day. Pause and let the mind relax and recover. Take a short walk or stretch break. Eat a healthy snack, drink plenty of water and breathe deeply.
- **Sleep On It**—If important decisions cannot be made in the morning, you may want to "sleep on it" and reconsider the decision the next morning.
- **Have Clear Goals**—Decision fatigue is linked to making complex choices from among alternatives. Be clear about your goals to minimize unnecessary choices and the drain on mental energy associated with decision-making.
- **Avoid Distractions**—Don't make decisions when distracted. It's become increasingly clear that we lessen our effectiveness when we try to balance multiple tasks at the same time. You can't avoid social media or email. But you can set specific times to tend to those tasks and avoid handling them when making other decisions. Turn off those automated alerts when a new email or text arrives.

Manage the Unexpected

Every principal has dealt with the unexpected. It might be an angry parent at the beginning of the school day, an urgent phone call from their supervisor, the crash of the platform for online learning or some inappropriate classroom activity.

The move to remote learning resulted in a lot of unexpected events, challenges that arose quickly and needed resolution. So, how do you handle the unexpected? Here's some advice culled from a variety of educational and business resources (Hunt, 2020; Vilhauer, 2016).

- **Pause Before Acting**—While some events may require immediate action, many of them benefit from taking a moment or two, or a day or two, to respond. The key is to be composed and have a very considered response. Never panic and act rashly. The evidence is that people will be less inclined to cooperate with you if you don't appear to be in control of yourself.
- **Trust It Will Turn Out Well**—Remember the times that something unexpected happened and you were successful in overcoming the problem. You might even look at the unexpected problem as an opportunity for you to show initiative and demonstrate how you cope under pressure.
- **Consult Others**—While an unexpected event can allow you to demonstrate your leadership, it is often helpful to consult with others. They may have skills or information that could help with resolving the problem. Seek help when appropriate; it's okay to ask for a second opinion. Just don't blame others if their advice doesn't prove helpful.
- **Evaluate and Learn**—Take time after every unexpected event to reflect on what happened. Identify the factors that contributed to the event, how you handled it and ways you might have handled it more effectively.
- **Expect and Accept the Unexpected**—There's always the possibility of the unexpected and no way to avoid it. While that can be unsettling, you can also accept it as just part of being a principal. Have confidence in your ability to weather the event and learn from the experience.

Managing Privacy When Working Remotely

A significant concern about working remotely is the privacy of information. Documents can be left visible on home computers or tablets. Data about students can reside on a teacher's desktop. Video conferences or Zoom lessons raise privacy issues about what others may see via your webcam. Students may be concerned about how to access school counselors or social workers for private conversations.

Several protocols have emerged for dealing with privacy in a remote work environment. Here are some of the most common recommendations.

- Establish a clear protocol for handling data when working remotely. Inform your employees of your security expectations. Assure that student data are password protected, and expect that teachers and other staff will not leave student data visible when away from their computer.
- Provide employees with a secure work computer that they can use rather than using their personal computer.
- Make sure employees work through a secure connection.
- Establish a remote learning code of conduct. Be clear about expectations around chat box comments or taking screenshots of virtual meetings.
- Keep online communities password protected.
- Never share more information than necessary.
- If you use Dropbox or Google Drive uploads, know who you can view your documents. Be familiar with everyone using a shared folder.
- Agree on the time for all video calls. Calls at unexpected or inappropriate times may be seen as an invasion of privacy. Be clear about when employees can be reached.
- Make virtual backgrounds available for students and staff who may be uncomfortable showing their home or current setting on the screen.
- Start meetings or classes by checking in with students or staff. Check for comfort before starting any conversation that might raise privacy concerns.

Final Thoughts

Few jobs are as complex as that of a principal. Principals deal with everything, including student safety, instructional supervision, budgeting and personnel. The onset of the pandemic and the move to remote learning added a level of complexity that was unexpected. However, if you do not focus on your own needs and the development of your leadership skills, you will not be as effective as you would like.

Points to Ponder

How does this information apply to my current situation?
What are two to three key points to remember?
What is one action step I would like to take?

References

Allen, D. (2001). *Getting things done: The art of stress-free productivity*. Viking.
Anderson, A. (2013). Work-life balance: 5 ways to turn it from the ultimate oxymoron into a real plan. *Forbes Magazine*. www.forbes.com/sites/amyanderson/2013/07/26/work-life-balance-the-ultimate-oxymoron-or-5-tips-to-help-you-achieve-better-worklife-balance/#6ac4b7bc5841
Blackburn, B. (2020). *Rigor in the remote learning classroom: Instructional tips and strategies*. Routledge.
Chakravarty, D. (2011). Working out the balance. *Business Today*. www.businesstoday.in/moneytoday/careers/right-balance-professional-and-personal-life/story/16457.html
Claessens, B., van Eerde, W., Rutte, C., & Roe, R. (2007). A review of the time management literature. *Time Management Literature*, 36(2), 255–270.
Covey, S. (1996). *First things first*. Simon & Schuster.
Graham, J. (2002). *Balancing work and family*. University of Maine. http://umaine.edu/publications/4186e/

Green, H. (2011). Avoiding the dreaded decision fatigue. *Forbes Magazine*. www.forbes.com/sites/work-in-progress/2011/09/07/avoiding-the-dreaded-decision-fatigue/

Haden, J. (2015). The best time management tool: Just say no. *Inc.com*. www.inc.com/jeff-haden/knowing-when-and-how-tosay-no.html

Hunt, S. (2020). A blueprint for dealing with the unexpected in work. *SkillsYouNeed*. www.skillsyouneed.com/rhubarb/dealing-with-unexpected-at-work.html#:~:text=A%20Blueprint%20for%20Dealing%20with%20the%20Unexpected%20in,will%20thrive%20and%20find%20ways%20to%20overcome%20adversity

Macan, T. H. (1994). Time management: Test of a process model. *Journal of Applied Psychology, 79*, 381–391.

Marshall, K. (2008). *The big rocks*. www.marshallmemo.com/articles/Time%20Management%20PL%20Mar%2008.pdf

McGregor, J. (2020). Remote work really does mean longer days—and more meetings. *Washington Post*. www.washingtonpost.com/business/2020/08/04/remote-work-longer-days/

Moregenstern, J. (2005). *Never check e-mail in the morning and other unexpected strategies for making your work life work*. Fireside Publishing.

Uscher, J. (2011). 5 tips for better work-life balance. *WebMD*. www.webmd.com/health-insurance/protect-health-13/balance-life

Vilhauer, J. (2016). 4 ways to survive unexpected situations. *Psychology Today*. www.psychologytoday.com/us/blog/living-forward/201605/4-ways-survive-unexpected-situations

Whitaker, K. (1996). Exploring causes of principal burnout. *Journal of Educational Administration, 34*(1), 60–71.

Williamson, R., & Blackburn, B. (2016). *The principalship from A to Z* (2nd ed.). Routledge.

Williamson, R., & Blackburn, B. (2019). *Seven strategies for improving your school*. Routledge.

References

Abrams, Z. (2020). Psychologists' advice for newly remote workers. *American Psychological Association.* www.apa.org/news/apa/2020/03/newly-remote-workers

Allen, D. (2001). *Getting things done: The art of stress-free productivity.* Viking.

Anderson, A. (2013). Work-life balance: 5 ways to turn it from the ultimate oxymoron into a real plan. *Forbes Magazine.* www.forbes.com/sites/amyanderson/2013/07/26/work-life-balance-the-ultimate-oxymoron-or-5-tips-to-help-you-achieve-better-worklife-balance/#6ac4b7bc5841

Barnes, F. (2004). *Inquiry and action: Making school improvement part of daily practice.* Annenberg Institute for School Reform at Brown University.

Barnum, M., & Bryan, C. (2020). America's great remote-learning experiment: Surveys of teachers and parents. *eSchoolNewt.* www.eschoolnews.com/2020/07/22/americas-great-remote-learning-experiment-what-surveys-of-teachers-and-parents-tell-us-about-how-it-went/#:~:text=%E2%80%9CAmerica%E2%80%99s%20great%20remote-learning%20experiment%3A%20What%20surveys%20of%20teachers,Chalkbeat%2C%20a%20nonprofit%20news%20organization%20covering%20public%20education

Blackburn, B. (2020). *Rigor in the remote learning classroom: Instructional tips and strategies.* Routledge.

Blackburn, R., Blackburn, B., & Williamson, R. (2018). *Advocacy from A to Z.* Routledge.

Bolman, L., & Deal, T. E. (2017). *Reframing organizations: Artistry, choice and leadership* (6th ed.). John Wiley & Sons, Inc.

Bower, M. (1996). *Will to manage.* McGraw Hill.

Chakravarty, D. (2011). Working out the balance. *Business Today.* www.businesstoday.in/moneytoday/careers/right-balance-professional-and-personal-life/story/16457.html

Claessens, B., van Eerde, W., Rutte, C., & Roe, R. (2007). A review of the time management literature. *Time Management Literature, 36*(2), 255–270.

Collaborative for Academic, Social, Emotional Learning. (2020). Core SEL competencies. *CASEL*. https://casel.org/core-competencies/

Collins, J. (2009). *How the mighty fall*. Harper Collins.

Covey, S. (1996). *First things first*. Simon & Schuster.

Dhawan, E., & Chamorro-Premuzic, T. (2018). *How to collaborate effectively if your team is remote*. https://hbr.org/2018/02/how-to-collaborate-effectively-if-your-team-is-remote

Education Trust. (2020). 10 questions for equity advocates to ask about distance learning. *Education Trust*. https://edtrust.org/resource/10-questions-for-equity-advocates-to-ask-about-distance-learning/

Gallo, A. (2016). How to manage a toxic employee. *Harvard Business Review*. https://hbr.org/2016/10/how-to-manage-a-toxic-employee

Garmston, R., & Wellman, B. (2013). *The adaptive school: A sourcebook for developing collaborative groups* (2nd ed.). Christopher-Gordon.

Glickman, C., Gordon, S., & Ross-Gordon, J. (2018). *Supervision and instructional leadership: A developmental approach* (10th ed.). Pearson.

Goleman, D. (2005). *Emotional intelligence: Why it can matter more than IQ*. Bantam Books.

Graham, J. (2002). *Balancing work and family*. University of Maine. http://umaine.edu/publications/4186e/

Green, H. (2011). Avoiding the dreaded decision fatigue. *Forbes Magazine*. www.forbes.com/sites/work-in-progress/2011/09/07/avoiding-the-dreaded-decision-fatigue/

Haden, J. (2015). The best time management tool: Just say no. *Inc.com*. www.inc.com/jeff-haden/knowing-when-and-how-to-say-no.html

Hattie, J. (2018). 252 influences and effect sizes related to student achievement. *Visible Learning*. https://visible-learning.org/hattie-ranking-influences-effect-sizes-learning-achievement/

Higgins, J. (2020). COVID has made rural schools suddenly responsible for getting internet to kids in remote, unserved areas. *Charlottesville Tomorrow.* www.cvilletomorrow.org/articles/covid-has-made-rural-schools-suddenly-responsible-for-getting-internet-to-kids-in-remote-unserved-areas/

Hirsh, S., & Killion, J. (2007). *The learning educator: A new era for professional learning.* Learning Forward.

Hoffman, J., Brackett, M., & Levy, S. (2020). How to foster a positive school climate in a virtual world. *EdSurge.* www.edsurge.com/news/2020-05-21-how-to-foster-a-positive-school-climate-in-a-virtual-world

Hooker, C. (2020). 5 ways to support parents during remote learning. *Tech & Learning.* www.techlearning.com/features/5-ways-to-support-parents-during-remote-learning#:~:text=Districts%20have%20deployed%20these%20five%20strategies%20to%20ways,schedules%2C%20platforms%2C%20and%20expectations%20for%20students%20and%20families

Hoy, W., & Tarter, C. (2008). *Administrators solving the problems of practice: Decision-making concepts, cases and consequences* (3rd ed.). Pearson Education.

Hubbard, L. (2020). 9 ways to tame anxiety during the COVID-19 pandemic. *Mayo Clinic.* www.mayoclinichealthsystem.org/hometown-health/speaking-of-health/9-ways-to-tame-anxiety-during-the-covid-19-pandemic

Hunt, S. (2020). A blueprint for dealing with the unexpected in work. *SkillsYouNeed.* www.skillsyouneed.com/rhubarb/dealing-with-unexpected-at-work.html#:~:text=A%20Blueprint%20for%20Dealing%20with%20the%20Unexpected%20in,will%20thrive%20and%20find%20ways%20to%20overcome%20adversity

Johnston, J. H., & Williamson, R. (2014). *Leading schools in an era of declining resources.* Routledge.

Kelly, M. (2020). 5 keys to being a successful teacher. *ThoughtCo.* www.thoughtco.com/keys-to-being-a-successful-teacher-8420

Kotter, J. (2008). *A sense of urgency.* Harvard Business School Publishing.

Kotter, J. (2012). *Leading change.* Harvard Business Review Press.

Larson, B., Vroman, S., & Makarius, E. (2020). A guide to managing your (newly) remote workers. *Harvard Business Review.* https://hbr.org/2020/03/a-guide-to-managing-your-newly-remote-workers

Markham, L. (2020). Coping with fear in the face of a pandemic. *Psychology Today.* www.psychologytoday.com/us/blog/peaceful-parents-happy-kids/202003/coping-fear-in-the-face-pandemic

McCan, T. H. (1994). Time management: Test of a process model. *Journal of Applied Psychology, 79,* 381–391.

McGregor, J. (2020). Remote work really does mean longer days—and more meetings. *Washington Post.* www.washingtonpost.com/business/2020/08/04/remote-work-longer-days/

Moregenstern, J. (2005). *Never check e-mail in the morning and other unexpected strategies for making your work life work.* Fireside Publishing.

National School Public Relations Association. (2020). *A guidebook for opinion leader/key communicator programs.* NSPRA.

Nawaz, S. (2020). How managers can support remote employees. *Harvard Business Review.* https://hbr.org/2020/04/how-managers-can-support-remote-employees

Oxley, D., Barton, R., & Klump, J. (2006). Creating small learning communities. *Principal's Research Review, 1*(6), 3.

Peterson, K. D., & Deal, T. E. (2002). *The shaping school culture fieldbook.* Jossey-Bass.

Petrilli, M. (2012). *How districts can stretch the school dollar.* Fordham Institute.

Porath, C. (2016). *Mastering civility: A manifesto for the workplace.* Grand Centeral Publishing.

Schein, E. (2016). *Organizational culture and leadership* (5th ed.). Jossey-Bass.

Talking Points. (2020). *Supporting high needs students and families with distance learning.* https://talkingpts.org/supporting-high-need-students-and-families-with-distance-learning/1812/

Uscher, J. (2011). 5 tips for better work-life balance. *WebMD.* www.webmd.com/health-insurance/protect-health-13/balance-life

Vilhauer, J. (2016). 4 ways to survive unexpected situations. *Psychology Today*. www.psychologytoday.com/us/blog/living-forward/201605/4-ways-survive-unexpected-situations

Whitaker, K. (1996). Exploring causes of principal burnout. *Journal of Educational Administration, 34*(1), 60–71.

Williamson, R., & Blackburn, B. (2016). *The principalship from A to Z* (2nd ed.). Routledge.

Williamson, R., & Blackburn, B. (2020a). *7 strategies for improving your school*. Routledge.

Williamson, R., & Blackburn, B. (2020b, Summer). Sustaining your school's culture in uncertain times. *TEPSA Leader, 33*(3).

Williamson, R., & Johnston, J. H. (2012). *The school leader's guide to social media*. Eye on Education.

For Product Safety Concerns and Information please contact our EU representative GPSR@taylorandfrancis.com
Taylor & Francis Verlag GmbH, Kaufingerstraße 24, 80331 München, Germany

www.ingramcontent.com/pod-product-compliance
Lightning Source LLC
Chambersburg PA
CBHW051524230426
43668CB00012B/1732